Two Among *the*
Righteous Few
Second Edition

Les and Lil,

Thank you for your interest in
this special story.

Best regards,

Marty Brounstein

Leah "Iweke" Baars

Two Among *the*
Righteous Few

Second Edition

A Story of Courage
in the Holocaust

Marty Brounstein

TATE PUBLISHING
AND ENTERPRISES, LLC

Published by Tate Publishing & Enterprises, LLC
127 E. Trade Center Terrace | Mustang, Oklahoma 73064 USA
1.888.361.9473 | www.tatepublishing.com

Tate Publishing is committed to excellence in the publishing industry. The company reflects the philosophy established by the founders, based on Psalm 68:11,
"The Lord gave the word and great was the company of those who published it."

Book design copyright © 2016 by Tate Publishing, LLC. All rights reserved.
Cover design by April Marciszewski
Interior design by Sarah Kirchen

Published in the United States of America
ISBN: 978-1-68352-453-3
1. History / Holocaust
2. History / Europe / Western
16.06.22

This book is dedicated to the memory of Frans and Mien Wijnakker. To your selfless acts of courage, I am eternally grateful.

This book is also dedicated to the memory of Louis and Lynn Baars and Cyril and Goldie Brounstein—two sets of parents I wish I could share this story with live. They would have been proud.

Lastly, this book is dedicated to the source of inspiration who encouraged and supported me to make this book become a reality. She's one of the key figures in the story—Baby Ineke, or Ineke Baars, as she was known by her Dutch acquaintances in the Netherlands, Leah Baars as she is commonly known today. I'm just the lucky person who also gets to call her wife.

Acknowledgments

Much of the historical account that shapes first and now second editions of this book comes from a self-published Dutch book titled *Enkelen Van De Enkelen,* translated to mean the *Few of the Few.* It was put together by Willie van Tongeren, the brother-in-law of Irene Wijnakker's daughter, Simone. Irene is the youngest of the five children of Frans and Mien. She is the keeper of this family history record that is based on audiotapes Frans Wijnakker made a year or so before his death in 1994 so his story from the war could be documented. Nellie Kolenbrander, the eldest of the five Wijnakker children, served as the point person from the family in providing greater insight into this remarkable story. She has also been our host in subsequent visits to the area since the initial and accidental visit of May 2009, described in Chapter One, that triggered the first edition to happen. A major assistance for getting valuable inside information was also provided by Shulamit Schwarz, a.k.a. Freetje, the first person Frans and Mien took into hiding. My wife and I have met her in person in Haifa, Israel. She is a strong and vibrant 88 years old as this second edition comes out. My wonderful wife, Leah Baars, also provided valuable assistance, from Dutch translation to historical background.

Thanks too to the staff at Tate Publishing for for this second edition; in particular, Marketing Consultant, Cody Crawford, and Christina Hicks, Director of Design, and her staff who helped put together this newest edition, plus April Marciszewski for her poignant book cover design.

A big thank you also goes out to the many supporters I've met along this unexpected journey in sharing this special story of courage, compassion, and rescue. Their help and encouragement have led to this second edition happening and the journey in telling this story continuing long past what most authors do with their books.

A special thanks goes to the five children of Frans and Mien Wijnakker—Nellie, Jan, Thijs, Frans, Jr., and Irene—for allowing and encouraging this writer to take this story forward.

Table of Contents

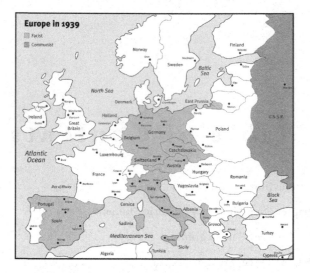

EUROPE IN 1939 PRIOR TO THE START OF WORLD WAR II.

EUROPE UNDER NAZI DOMINATION BY THE END OF 1941.

THE PROVINCE OF NORTH BRABANT IN
HOLLAND AND SOME OF THE MAIN TOWNS
WHERE FRANS DID HIS SPECIAL BUSINESS.

Introduction

I want to take you on a journey into a remarkable story, and to start this journey I want you to think about these three questions. Question one: Would you be willing to help others whose lives are in great danger? Question two: Would you be willing to help others whose lives are in great danger, knowing if you get involved, you probably put your life in great danger. Would you still help? And question three: Would you be willing to help others whose lives are in great danger, knowing if you get involved you probably put your life in great danger, when these people who most need the help most everyone else wants to hate them or be indifferent to their plight. Would you still get involved and help?

Two Among the Righteous Few: A Story of Courage in the Holocaust is a true story of a Christian couple from the Netherlands who answered a definite yes to all three of those questions in a time period when most everyone else said no. They are true heroes.

This has been the opening to my storytelling presentation about this remarkable husband and wife named Franciscus and Hermina Wijnakker, Frans and Mien for short (pronounced like Franz and Mean)—an opening audiences find quite thought-provoking. At the writing of this second edition for the book, this unexpected journey of sharing this special story with a wide variety of audiences and venues is now five years and counting. I often tell audiences that this is a story I stumbled into by accident on a trip to the Netherlands with my wife in May 2009.

My wife's curiosity led us to connect with the five children of Frans and Mien, a reconnection for my wife. On this initial accidental visit to the home of Frans Wijnakker, Jr., who lives in the actual house where much of his parents' rescue work occurred, I was blown away when I learned that his parents had been recognized as Righteous Among the Nations. I knew what this honor meant.

Nestled up in the hills on the western side of the city of Jerusalem is a place where thousands of people from around the world visit daily to learn about the tragic period of history from 1933 to 1945 known as the Holocaust. The name of this place is Yad Vashem. It was established in 1953 by an act of the Knesset, Israel's parliament, to serve as an education, research, and historical center in remembrance of the six million Jews who were murdered in the Holocaust at the hands of the Nazi Party machine led by Adolf Hitler.

That number, six million, can be almost unimaginable to the average person. What it means in terms of the Holocaust is that nearly two-thirds of the Jewish population that existed in Europe prior to the start of World War II perished at the hands of the Nazis and their collaborators by war's end in May 1945. These were targeted victims of murder, not victims of war where millions more soldiers and civilians died from the most destructive war in humankind's history. The Holocaust also included another five million-plus murdered victims on Hitler's list of so-called inferiors and undesirables, such as gypsies, the handicapped, homosexuals, political opponents and dissidents, and those of Slavic heritage.

So this tragedy would never be forgotten is why Yad Vashem was created. Amidst the many parts of this fascinating historical museum is a section called the Righteous Among the Nations, a section that recognizes the non-Jews, who carried out acts of courage to save the lives of Jews during the Holocaust. On the grounds outside the walls of the museum are plaques and planted trees that pay tribute to these courageous people, the area often referred to as the Avenue of the Righteous. In fact, the 1993 Academy Award winning movie *Schindler's List* featured one of the best known of these Righteous few, Oskar Schindler. Another 26,000-plus as of the start of 2016 Righteous people who have received this special honor from Yad Vashem join him.

The actions these people took to help Jews included creating papers for false identities, hiding them, helping them get away, or providing other means of refuge. Such actions may be hard for some to grasp as daring and bold if absorbed in the world of today with its high-action, high-drama movies, video games, and sensationalized stories in the media and Internet or the misused word of hero that gets attached to celebrities in the world of sports and entertainment.

Make no mistake about it; everyone recognized in Yad Vashem's Avenue of the Righteous truly participated in real-life drama that put his or her life at great risk. The ugly scourge of anti-Semitism was not just confined to Adolf Hitler's Germany in the 1930s and 1940s. By the start of 1942 Germany and its allies in the Axis Powers had conquered most of the countries of Europe outside of Great Britain and the Soviet Union, with much of the European portion of the U.S.S.R. overrun by German forces. In most every one of these countries, the Nazis found sympathizers who gladly assisted them in the brutalizing, murdering, or rounding up of Jews to be shipped off to the concentration camps in Poland and elsewhere. Of course, millions more chose to look the other way or were just indifferent to the plight of Jews among their citizenry.

On top of this setting was the brutality the Nazi henchman carried out to anyone caught trying to help save Jews. Death was the outcome in quite a few cases either on the spot by being beaten to death, burned to death, or shot, or if one was lucky enough to just be arrested, the concentration camp was usually the destination with dying either in the gas chambers or through backbreaking labor and starvation the most common outcome.

In light of this hostile climate at that time in Europe (and elsewhere around the world) and the dangerous risks involved, the actions of this small minority of non-Jews recognized by Yad Vashem were truly remarkable and courageous. These Righteous people were truly heroes. In Section H on the grounds in the Avenue of the Righteous, you will find the plaque of two such people, a couple from a small town in the Netherlands named Franciscus and Hermina Wijnakker.

This book tells the story of this Christian couple, commonly referred to as Frans and Mien, and the actions they took in the time of the Holocaust that eventually earned them this special honor at Yad Vashem. Among the many heroic acts Frans and Mien performed was taking into hiding in their own home a young Jewish couple similar in age to them where the wife was already pregnant. They performed a miracle and got this baby born and kept her safe—the wife of this very author.

Please enjoy the journey ahead.

Chapter One:
May 2009 Historic
Moment

Subject: Historic Moment
Date: May 26, 2009, 10:25 a.m.
Dear Shoshana and Alana,

Today is Tuesday, May 26, 2009. I am writing to share more than just travel stories from a wonderful journey your mom and I are having. I want to document something to you that I hope you will find of much value for your own family history.

While I know some of the history, and you probably do too, coming in contact with the reality of it merges mind and heart into something of great significance. I will explain shortly.

Being in the Netherlands, much more than in the United States, one is reminded of World War II and the Holocaust as well. When we started our trip in Amsterdam, we visited the Anne Frank house. It is a wonderful educational museum. Last Friday, we visited the museum and site of Camp Westerbork. Before World War II, there were 140,000 Jews who lived in the Netherlands. One hundred seven thousand, over seventy-five percent, perished during the Holocaust. Westerbork was the deportation center the Nazis used to ship the Dutch Jews off to the death camps in Poland, mostly Auschwitz and Sobibor.

We arrived last evening in the city of Eindhoven in the south of the country. Of the places your mom's family lived prior to immigrating to the U.S., Eindhoven was where they were the longest. Before arriving there yesterday, we stopped in an old town named Ravenstein. It is the big small town in an area of villages in a southern section of the Netherlands. It is also near where your grandparents, Opa and Oma, were hidden during the war.

As we stop and walk around the charming 1600s historic downtown of Ravenstein, all two blocks of it, we spot a tourist information office. We go in, and your mom asks the staff members about the location of an old church in the nearby small town of Dieden and if the home that once belonged to a Frans Wijnakker is still next to it. For the older folks of this area, which the three office people on hand were, the name of Frans Wijnakker is a notable one.

They tell your mom not only how to get to this church but also that one of the Wijnakker sons still lives in this particular house. In addition, one of the office people gives your mom an e-mail address that she can contact to get a self-published Dutch book that was written about Frans Wijnakker and his story during World War II. So off we go down the road to Dieden. About ten minutes later, we find the vacant church in question. Old churches in Holland often go back anywhere from 300 to 900 years and are very noticeable by their towers, which are sometimes a few stories high.

We park our car at the old church and walk over to the house next door. The house has a long driveway. As we walk up the driveway, we see a few people sitting at a table in the front yard on this warm day, and we see the word *Shalom* written on the front side of the house, probably a foot in size. Your mom boldly walks up to the gentleman sitting there and says in Dutch, "Hello, I'm Ineke Baars." A roar goes up along with a warm handshake. This man and his wife sitting with him know who Ineke Baars is and much more of the significance related to her. In the next few minutes, the Dutch starts flying and phone calls start happening. Within ten minutes, his youngest sibling, Irene, drives over and joins in the lively discussion.

The man who has greeted us is Frans Wijnakker, Jr. He is the youngest son of the aforementioned Frans Wijnakker. His father, Frans, with the support of his mother, Mien, saved your grandparents and your mom, Baby Ineke, during World War II. They all survived the Holocaust because this Catholic man and his wife hid them and other Jews and helped even more hide from the Nazis. *Do you recognize the significance of this moment!* My wife, who is so good to me, and your mother, who loves you two so dearly, would not be here today if it were not for the parents of these two siblings sitting in front of us talking to your mom as if she was their long-lost half sister.

As a child, your mom and her family would travel to Dieden each summer to visit the Wijnakker family. Then twenty-five years ago, the last time your mom visited the Netherlands, with five-year-old Shoshana, she came to a special event in Ravenstein. Yad Vashem, the Holocaust memorial museum in Israel, had selected Frans and Mien Wijnakker as Righteous Gentiles who helped save Jews during the Holocaust. Local officials and townspeople put on a ceremony and parade for Frans to recognize this honor he'd been given. Opa helped fund a trip for Frans a few months after that so he could be honored in person at Yad Vashem in Jerusalem. His wife, Mien, passed away in 1980. Frans passed away in 1994.

Frans, the son, and his wife, also named Irene, visited Israel themselves last year. They showed us a blown-up picture of the memorial plaque and tree planted in Yad Vashem's Avenue of the Righteous section in honor of their parents, which was when the historic significance of what I was witnessing really hit me! Irene, the sister, then gave your mom the special book mentioned to us at the tourist office about their father and his story during World War II. While I merely can just watch the conversation because it's all in Dutch, I can still follow what's happening along with occasional translations your mom provides. After visiting for over an hour, they have invited us to come back Wednesday evening. They have three other siblings who are all alive, and living in the local area, each with their own children and grandchildren. So your mom will likely meet more of the Wijnakker family who she last saw twenty-five years ago.

We are in the midst of reading this self-published book about Frans and Mien Wijnakker. Actually, it is in Dutch, so your mom reads and translates to me. This man of simple means and small-town living along with a wife of great strength turn out to become a couple of great courage, risk taking, and compassion. Your grandparents are talked about in this book among many of the others who Frans and Mien helped save. Later in the book, it tells of a baby born to the Baars couple who the Wijnakkers take as their own to help save her. You know quite well the special person this baby became.

Pretty neat piece of history! I hope you can appreciate this historic moment I have shared.

Love,
Marty

Chapter Two:
The Beginning

Franciscus Wijnakker was born August 31, 1908, and Hermina van de Coolwijk was born June 14, 1913. Both were products of large Catholic families. Frans was one of eleven children, and Mien was one of ten. Both were born and raised in the small town of Haren located in the province of North Brabant (usually referred to as Brabant) in the southern part of the nation of the Netherlands, commonly referred to as Holland. Haren was a farming village where people raised cows and crops. The area was relatively poor, and life was meager as a result. Going off to college for further education was not part of the lifestyle for the people of this area.

From these humble beginnings, Frans and Mien, as they were commonly called, married on January 16, 1936. He was a man slight of build and stature, approximately five feet seven inches, and she was nearly the same height. As young adults in their twenties, they were relatively fit and not overweight—nothing stunning to look at but not unattractive either. Their desires in life were simple: work hard, be good Catholics, and raise a family.

They made their home in the nearby town of Dieden, situated on the Maas River. Together with Demen, its closest neighboring village, there lived a few hundred people. Dieden was rather isolated. There was no bus, and not everyone had a bicycle, as was common throughout much of the country. If a car came through, children often came running to the street to watch it go by.

The largest town in the area, about ten miles away, was Oss. The closest town in the general community where the train came through was Ravenstein, a couple of miles or so from Dieden.

In this small village and agricultural area, most of the residents, like the Wijnakker couple, were Roman Catholic. In those days, the priest held a very prominent position in the community and was very much looked up to as a person of authority. In the spirit of that time, the 1930s, there was the mayor, the notary, the head teacher, and the priest as the key local authority figures. The priest, usually the most educated person in the area, had many roles in the community. He sat on the church and school boards, on the board of directors of the Farm Loan Bank, and he was often the advisor for local organizations. In brief, he was involved in everything.

After their wedding, Frans and Mien made their home in an old parsonage that had previously been the home of a Protestant minister. They rented this large house from the Netherlands Reformed Church, whose offices were some miles away, as Dieden no longer had its own Protestant minister. Next to the parsonage stood its church, an old church from the eleventh century. The church was close to being in ruins and was not in operation. The tower had no steeple, and the church's roof was mostly missing. The parsonage stood against the south side of the embankment of the Maas River, which streamed by a few hundred yards to the north.

Upon moving into their house, Frans and Mien wanted to hang a crucifix in it. Mien asked a neighbor how this effort worked in Dieden and learned the cross had to be first blessed by the parish priest. "The cross should lie on a table with a holy statue next to it and also some holy water and a small palm branch. Then the priest can bless it. Also get some cognac. The priest likes a cognac and a cigar," the neighbor told her.

Thus, the Wijnakkers invited the priest, Father Johannes Simons, to come to their house to bless the cross. Father Simons had, of course, never been in the house since Protestants had always occupied it before. He did not think much of the fact that the Wijnakkers would live in a Protestant parsonage, saying to Frans, "I don't understand why you are going to live in this house. From olden days, Protestants have lived here. From father to son, they were all Protestants. Now a Catholic comes to live here. You are a Catholic, right?"

"Yes," Frans replied.

"Then I think," the priest said as he pointed to the crucifix, "he won't adjust well in this house. A cross has never hung here before."

Somewhat irritated, Frans answered, "Father, go ahead and bless him. He will hang there, and if he can't adjust, then he'll leave."

That remark was not received well. Father Simons did not say anything. He picked up the palm branch, blessed the cross, and left—without the drink and without the cigar. Frans always felt the blessing counted anyway.

Father Simons was not impressed with his new parishioners. Some time later when Frans went to confession, the priest said to him, "Wijnakker, I've seen something terrible, something that cannot be accepted. Every year the topic is talked about. Covering to the elbows and with a closed neck is important for women to do. Was it not like that in Haren?"

Father Simons had been seriously upset by the fact that Mien had recently come to communion in a dress with an open neckline. That was viewed as a sin. Frans just smiled and said little in response.

✳

Frans worked as a miller in the grain milling business of the Meulemans in Ravenstein. He had learned the trade from an uncle in the town of Schayk. It was normal in those days to learn a trade from someone in your family.

At the same time, as the decade of the 1930s wore on, the threat of war was looming again. Adolf Hitler had risen to power in Germany, and a military buildup was well under way. As 1939 began Hitler had already worked his way with the powers of Europe at that time, Great Britain and France, annexing Austria and being granted a portion of Czechoslovakia. In March 1939 Hitler had Germany annex the rest of Czechoslovakia. British Prime Minister Neville Chamberlain's policy of appeasement with the German dictator was in tatters. Then on the first of September 1939, World War II had begun in Europe with Germany's attack on Poland. Britain and France declared war against Germany two days later, much to the joy and excitement of the Polish people. But military help from these so-called powers to fight against Germany would not appear. Within a month, Poland had succumbed.

For people in Holland, the threat of Nazi Germany grew more and more. Holland had remained neutral in World War I and had declared in its neutrality again, along with its neighboring country to the south, Belgium. The likelihood of Germany honoring that neutrality grew less and less. With Germany now at war against Britain, the seas began to become dangerous for ships to travel. German mines and u-boats were in full force. On November 18, 1939 the Dutch passenger liner Simon Bolivar sailing from Holland to England ran into German mines in the North Sea near Harwich, England. The ship sank with 400 passengers and crew on board, with over 80 people dying in the incident including the ship's captain.

The major country of Germany covered the eastern border of the Netherlands. With Germany's growing aggressive actions in the 1930s and its movement into war, the Dutch government was wondering how long its small nation would be left alone. The Dutch military began to prepare.

Since the Wijnakkers had a large house, they were willing to quarter Dutch soldiers there. These soldiers came from various parts of the Netherlands, including from the more urban western parts. The priest was worried about the wrong kind of influences on the community, thinking these city-type characters might pass on their sinful ways to the small-town folk of the area.

Frans, who regularly attended church, got to hear about this at confession one day in the fall of 1939. Before Frans could offer his confession, Father Simons anxiously blurted out to him, "Now I've heard something awful. You don't know about it, as you were not home. At least I think not. You were probably working in the mill. I heard that there was a window open at your house."

The local government had ordered that the shutters be kept closed. For saftety reasons, residents throughout the country were told to keep their curtains and shutters closed. The thinking was that conditions would be safer for homes if they looked closed rather than open should a German attack occur.

The priest continued. "I discussed this with the commander. The soldiers are to be in the back of the house, not in the front of the house. There are thirty quartered soldiers with you, and they were seen in the large living room, the windows open, all of them sitting inside, and your wife was serving them coffee. She was serving those young men while dancing through the house. Terrible, you don't know what types you have in your house. No beliefs, or maybe Protestant. It's terrible!"

"I'll mention it at home," Frans answered in his laconic way. The incident was actually minor but had been blown up through the rumor mill in the community to which the priest was closely connected.

Frans got to know the soldiers that were quartered in his house, and these contacts proved to be useful even long after they departed. Later on during the war, Frans would take a leave of absence from his job at the grain mill. He would get into a black market business of selling meat, fat, and eggs. He would travel to the major cities in the western part of the country, including Amsterdam, because of the contacts he had made while the soldiers had been quartered in his house.

While Frans earned fairly good money with his business of selling meat and eggs in the western cities, the family still needed to live frugally. Frans sometimes still worked as a miller for the granary in town to help make ends meet. He wanted to one day build his own windmill and become an independent mill owner.

Then May 10, 1940, came. German forces invaded the Netherlands. The Dutch put up a fight, with its army taking on the powerful German forces. The British and French attempted to send in troops to help, but no useful coordination occurred, leaving the Dutch military on its own. In fact, mighty France would come under attack ten days later and would surrender in less than a month. Poor Holland would surrender in less than one week.

While the Dutch forces were putting up a good fight, which the German commanders did not like, the Germans turned to the Dutch government and issued an ultimatum.

Either surrender now or the Germans would start bombing, going after the major commercial port city of Rotterdam first. The Dutch prime minister, Dirk Jan de Geer, in consultation with his cabinet and with the queen, Queen Wilhelmina, did not want this destruction to occur on their land. So they ordered their commanding general to negotiate surrender terms with the Germans, who gladly accepted. Yet, in what the Germans termed a miscommunication, Rotterdam got bombed to smithereens anyway. 1,000 people were killed, 85,000 left homeless, and the industrial center of the city wiped out.

A day before the official surrender Queen Wilhelmina and her royal family, along with the prime minister and his cabinet, fled to Great Britain as a government in exile. They would spend the rest of the war there. In fact, within a month, by the end of June 1940, the Nazi blitzkrieg had toppled most of Northern and Western Europe, other than Great Britain. By June 1941, most of Europe had fallen under the control of Adolf Hitler's Germany and his Axis allies including Italy, Romania, Hungary, and Bulgaria. The few countries still allowed to be on the neutral list—Switzerland, Sweeden, Spain, Portugal, and Turkey—while not fighting were actively supplying the Germans with material needs for their war machine and hoping the Germans would not change their mind and attack them. Britain was shaken yet still standing, the United States was still sitting on the sidelines, and the Nazi attack on the Eastern front had been launched with the forces of the Soviet Union under retreat. By December of 1941, as the United States suffered the attack at Pearl Harbor to finally come into

World War II, German forces were within 20 miles of the capital of Moscow. The Soviet Union was near collapse and the rest of the continent was under the occupation of Germany or its Axis allies—possibly the most frightening time in the world's history.

Meanwhile, before May 1940 had concluded, Holland was now an occupied country, not knowing the pending disaster for itself or the rest of Europe to come soon. Arthur Seyss-Inquart, an Austrian Nazi, was put in charge as the ruling governor of this conquered land. He would surround himself with his own henchmen to run the country. The most brutal and feared among them was Hanns Albin Rauter, the head of the SS, the security arm of the Nazi machine to enforce its will on the people. The occupation of the Netherlands would last five miserable years, the longest and worst among the countries of Western Europe. The Nazi push to round up Jews, put them into ghettos, ship them off to concentration camps, and eventually exterminate them was on the horizon. The first Nazi raid to round up Jews and ship them off to concentration camps occurred in Amsterdam in late February 1941. By 1942, being rounded up to live in ghettos in Amsterdam and then get shipped off to concentration camps would become the norm for most Jews in Holland. Throughout 1941 edicts kept coming out from the German authorities in the Netherlands targeting Jews in the country. By the end of 1941, the result was the Jewish population had been isolated and removed from the non-Jewish population. Jews were no longer allowed to go to school with non-Jews, attend universities, or work with non-Jews. If you were a Jew who owned your own business, that was now taken away. If Jews wanted to go out and enjoy social and recreational activities like anyone else, they were now prohibited from doing so.

By May 1942 when Jews went out in public, they had to wear that yellow badge of humiliation on their clothing that identified them as a Jew. By July 1942 the trains were cranking. The Germans were taking the Jews out of the three districts set up as ghettos in Amsterdam, using the Hollandse Schouwberg, the main Dutch Theater of Amsterdam, as a depot center, and shipping them bit by bit primarily to the death camps in Poland, Sobibor and Auschwitz-Birkenau. The Nazis controlled the press and were masters of propaganda. The message they told the whole Dutch population, Jewish and non-Jewish alike, was that the Jews were being sent to work camps in Germany. False.

In the meantime, Frans did his best to maintain a normal life as much as possible despite the Netherlands falling under Nazi control. Living in the countryside rather than in the cities, Frans was less exposed to what life was like under the Nazi occupation. He kept up his business of selling meat and eggs. As part of doing business, he sometimes took trips to Amsterdam. He had customers there, and these customers had acquaintances, and hence Frans would then also go to meet them.

In 1942, around the time of the birth of his youngest son, Frans, Jr., he ran into a serious mishap. Frans was arrested by the Dutch police and jailed in the city of Den Bosch, accused of hoarding grain and possibly moon shining, forbidden activities especially during the war. The

Dutch authorities, wanting to stay on the good side of the Germans, were not buying his story that some travelers had left the grain with him for a short period. But Frans was not deterred as he persisted with his claims that this was all some misunderstanding. After a few months, he was released and allowed to go home. Mien and the four children, at the time, stayed in their home and made do, although worried and wondering when Frans would return home.

When Frans returned, he continued with his business trips through Holland to sell his goods of meat and eggs. This valuable food was now fairly scarce in the Netherlands, as the Germans had shipped much of it off to Germany to feed their own soldiers and people. What Frans was doing was actually a black market business, truly not legal. People in the cities were supposed to use German-mandated ration cards to get their food and supplies.

Frans was a good salesman with this risky business, and people in the cities were willing to pay for this scarce goods of food. On one such trip to Amsterdam in the spring of 1943, Frans came to the house of a doctor whom he had met previously in his business travels. His visit to the doctor that morning changed his life as he now came into contact with one of the large dramas of World War II: the persecution of the Jews.

"I heard from the woman upstairs that you live in a nice, quiet area. She said that there are only around three hundred people in your village in the neighborhood of Zaltbommel," the doctor said to Frans. The upstairs neighbor did not know any better, and she always said that Frans came from there. Frans spoke up to correct the doctor. "Actually I live in the small town of Dieden in Brabant."

"I want to ask you something," the doctor continued. "Could you take a girl with you? Could you take her for maybe up to three weeks to your town of Dieden? That way she could get a little better food and better fresh air. I have an acquaintance, and she has a girl in her house who is underfed. I said I would look for someone, and then we can send the girl out of the city for a bit. Oh, by the way, she's Jewish. So would you be willing to help?"

"Yes, for three weeks. That's okay. We have enough food," Frans responded in an easygoing and casual manner.

At this point, Frans was not fully aware of what was happening to Jews in Holland, nor of the dangers of Nazi occupation that people in the cities faced. The countryside where he lived had no Jewish residents and had little German Nazi presence at this time. For many of the Dutch at that time, if someone you know asks for your help and you can help, then you do so. This doctor was a casual acquaintance who had asked for helped; therefore, Frans said yes.

The doctor responded with a smile. "That's good. Would you like to see the girl first before you finish your business today and head back home with her?"

"If possible," Frans said.

The doctor gave Frans the address where he could meet the girl. He also let him know that he would get word to the woman there so she would know who he was when he arrived. A short time later, Frans went to the given address and knocked on the door. An elderly woman opened the door just a crack and stared at him.

"I come from the doctor," Frans said in his greeting to the woman, Mrs. Junkman.

"Come closer to the door and whisper to me what your business here is," directed Mrs. Junkman.

When Frans explained that he had come to help transport a young girl to a safe place where she could be well fed for a little while, Mrs. Junkman motioned for him to come into her house.

"Yes, you are that fellow I've been told about. I had to be sure that the person ringing the doorbell would be you. I'll go get the girl."

Then Mrs. Junkman opened a closet door. A thin girl of fourteen years old stood in the closet, although she looked younger due to her small size. At that time, to have a Jewish child hiding in one's home was quite dangerous, especially in the cities where the Nazi presence was the greatest along with Dutch Nazis and sympathizers to the Nazis. At this time, Frans was not too aware of these dangers.

"I'll take her with me later today," he said.

"What time?" she asked.

"About four."

"No, that won't work."

"How about I get her at eight?" Frans asked.

The woman, with a concerned look on her face, replied, "No, not then. There is still some light then. It has to be a little later. After sunset." She continued, "I want to ask you something. Didn't you find it strange that the child was in the closet?"

"Yes, I did," Frans answered.

She then asked, "Did the doctor tell you anything else?

"Not really," Frans responded. "He only asked if I would take a child with me for a few weeks."

"Let me fill you in on some things." Mrs. Junkman then explained to Frans, "This girl is Jewish. In fact, she is a German Jewish girl. She came here in 1938 after the German-Dutch border was opened briefly to let in a certain number of Jewish children but not adults. The Netherlands was not generous in allowing in Jewish refugees. 'The Netherlands was full' was often the line given. Our government was just too timid and didn't want to offend Germany. So the children who were let in, like this young girl, were placed with foster parents and even attended school."

The woman continued, "She's been given the Dutch name of Freetje. You'll take her anyway, won't you?"

Thinking the assistance was only for three weeks, Frans nodded yes.

"Now here are the instructions to follow: You will meet the girl at the Central Train Station just before nine this evening. Go stand under the clock. Put a newspaper in your right jacket pocket. When you enter the train, the child will follow you. The girl will sit at a distance, facing you. You're going to Zaltbommel, right?"

"No, I don't live in Zaltbommel. I actually live near Ravenstein."

Mrs. Junkman found a map and noted that Ravenstein was a little place with a small railway station. She then continued with her instructions. "I'll buy her a ticket to Den Bosch. Then when you get off there to transfer, assist her only if truly needed to buy a ticket to go on the train to

Ravenstein. This serves to give the impression that the trip did not start in Amsterdam. At no time should you sit with her, as that can be dangerous. She knows to stay in the last car away from you for the whole journey."

"Are there further costs you see?" Mrs. Junkman asked Frans.

"No," he replied. "It won't cost anything. She can lodge with us for free."

At the Central Station in Amsterdam, everything went off as agreed. When the train reached the first major city in the province of Brabant, Den Bosch, Frans and the young girl called Freetje both stepped off the train. They then transferred to a train headed to Ravenstein. Per instructions, Freetje started out sitting away from Frans as she had done in the first leg of the journey. With few passengers around, all was quiet in the train. After a while, Frans told the girl she could sit with him. That, in itself, added danger and went against the instructions. Meanwhile, when Frans was not home by supper time as he usually was, Mien began to worry. Did her husband get arrested for his black market business, she wondered. It was only a year ago that he ended up in jail for a risky venture. When the hours of the evening went by, her worry only grew. After getting the children into bed by nine o'clock, she sat anxiously looking out the front window while knitting to keep her hands busy.

Then Frans and Freejte finally arrived at the train station in Ravenstein. They walked from there to Dieden, about two miles away. By near midnight, they were finally home.

"You are late," said Mien, wide awake and looking worried.

"Yes," responded Frans. "I have a child with me. She is an acquaintance of the doctor I know in Amsterdam. The child needs outside air and needs to eat well to regain some of her weight."

"Is there not enough to eat where she was?"

Frans answered, "No, there wasn't, but we have enough food. And her stay is only for three weeks." Mien nodded her head in agreement. She then spoke softly, "Well it's late. Let's get her to bed," and helped Freetje settle into a bed so they could all get some sleep.

Freetje would be the first Jew to arrive and hide in the Wijnakker house. Her stay would not be as temporary as first thought. The mission to shelter Jews so they could escape from Nazi persecution had only just begun for Frans and Mien.

Chapter Three:
Freetje

Freetje DeGroot, the name stated on her Dutch identity card, was actually Shulamit Laub, or Shula for short. She had been given this Dutch name to hide the fact that she was a Jewish girl from Germany. Born May 12, 1928, she would turn fifteen shortly after arriving at the Wijnakker household.

Shula was the third oldest of six Laub children with a loving father and mother, Marcus and Berta Laub, living in Mainz, Germany. She came from a middle-class religious family whose life would be turned into one of fear and tragedy as first faced by German Jews with the rise of Nazism and Adolf Hitler in the 1930s and then by Jews throughout Europe during the years of World War II that ran from September 1939 into May 1945. In the end, what we know as the Holocaust would lead to the murder of nearly two-thirds of European Jewry at the time, some six million people, plus another five million of other so-called inferiors and undesirables according to Hitler and his Nazi Party.

Shula's father owned and ran a retail store in Germany. It was a family business, one he had taken over from his father, who started it after emigrating from Poland earlier in the twentieth century.

By January 1933, Hitler's decade-long effort to rise to power had been fulfilled. He was now appointed chancellor of Germany. By that April, any semblance of democracy was gone, and the Nazi dictatorship was in full control. The Jewish population in Germany at this time was approximately six hundred thousand, slightly less than one percent of the total German population.

Hitler's anti-Jewish rhetoric that characterized his campaign to gain power through the 1920s and early 1930s would now turn into action. In 1933, Jewish reporters and editors in the newspaper field were banned from working for any German press organization. Jews were barred from working in civil service positions and in university positions such as professors. Enrollment by Jews in universities would be greatly restricted. Nazi-organized book burning events sprung up, with works by Albert Einstein, Sigmund Freud, and other Jews extinguished in flames. The government also ordered a one-day national boycott of Jewish stores and businesses on April 1, 1933. Nazi thugs stood in front of these establishments to prevent people from entering them, beating some Jews as part of the process. In March 1933 the initial concentration camps of Dachau, Oranienburg, and Sachsenburg were set up. Within a few months 30,000 prisoners were housed in them—some

Jews, communists, and socialists. No political opposition to the Nazi regime would be allowed in any form.

The Nazi anti-Semitic push escalated in September 1935 with the passing of what was called the Nuremberg Laws on Citizenship and Race. These edicts stripped Jews of their German citizenship and right to vote. They were no longer allowed to attend German schools and universities. Going to libraries and theaters, as well as using public transportation, was now prohibited. Intermarriage between Jews and non-Jews, the so-called pure Germans Hitler referred to as Aryans, was also forbidden.

As the 1930s wore on, coming home from school for Shula sometimes meant running from other German children she could not attend school with, being chased amidst slurs and taunts that she was going to be killed. Shula's family coped and carried on as best they could under these very restrictive and hostile conditions.

The Nazi strategy of the 1930s was to isolate and remove Jews from everyday life in German society, hoping most would leave the country outright. Between the start of 1933 when Hitler came to power through the beginning of November 1938, 30 percent of the Jewish population of Germany had indeed uprooted and moved to other countries. Yet some Jews remained, hoping all this craziness would pass. Germany had always been their home, and some were veterans of the German army in World War I. For some other German Jews who did desire to get out, there was nowhere to go. Restrictive immigration quotas along with general indifference in westernized countries to the growing Jewish refugee problem meant the opportunity to get to other parts of Europe, Canada, the United States, or British-controlled Palestine was very limited to nonexistent.

Hitler grew impatient. While he was pleased in hosting the 1936 Olympics in Berlin and with the progress of the military buildup he was pushing in Germany, he was displeased with the pace of departure of Jews. In October 1938, Hitler ordered the deportation of Jews residing in Germany who were originally from Poland. The Schutzstaffel, commonly known by the initials SS, gladly went to work to meet the Fuhrer's demands. The SS, led by Heinrich Himmler, was the security apparatus of the Nazi machine. The SS not only ran the police, referred to as the Gestapo, but also took on the responsibility of hunting down and rounding up Jews and of running the concentration camps that became death camps when World War II broke out. The SS rounded up sixteen thousand such Jews of Polish origin and dumped them across the border in Poland, with the Polish authorities sending most of them back across the border into Germany. Stuck in this state of limbo with no provisions, many of these Jews were not heard from again. Among this group were Shula's paternal grandparents.

Then a short time later the most frightening event of all took place. On November 9, 1938, *Kristallnacht* occurred, translated to mean the "night of broken glass." Throughout Germany and Austria, now annexed by Germany earlier in 1938, a Nazi-staged massive attack against Jews erupted. Over the course of two days, many Jews were beaten and tortured and women were raped. Jewish businesses and stores were smashed up and looted and some homes as well. Synagogues were vandalized and set on fire. In the end, nearly a hundred Jews had been beaten to death, 191 synagogues were ravaged, and thirty thousand men rounded up and shipped off to the growing number of concentration camps set up in Germany. Among those men taken away was Marcus Laub, Shula's father.

A month later Shula's father was released from Buchenwald and returned home. He was told to get his family out of Germany by January 1. But without any connections to other countries, there was no place for the whole family to go. A small window of opportunity existed with the Netherlands, as the Dutch government was willing to take in a few thousand German Jewish children at this time—the term was unaccompanied children, not families.

In late December 1938, under the guise of going on a family vacation, Shula's father took his six children to the border of Holland and left them there. Their mother had been too emotionally wrought to come along for this trip.

The Laub children would never see their parents again. As the new year began in 1939, Shula, at age ten, was now an orphan. But at least she was with her siblings; her oldest brother, Leo, was fourteen; her oldest sister, Esther, was twelve; her younger brother, Avraham, was eight; and her younger sisters, Sara and Hannah, were seven and six, respectively. After a few weeks in quarantine for examination and six months in a children's camp, Shula and her five siblings were placed with various Jewish families in Amsterdam. They were able to stay in contact and often saw each other on the Sabbath.

Shula ended up with the Asscher family and was treated as another child in the family. She attended a Jewish day school and quickly learned Dutch.

For nearly a year, Shula lived a fairly normal life. She enjoyed going to school and no longer had to face taunts and ridicule from other children for being Jewish. She played with her friends after school, including one close in age who lived down the same block, a girl named Anne Frank.

However, by the start of June 1940, the danger started all over again and would turn out to be even worse. The Netherlands was now a conquered country under the control of Nazi Germany. Throughout 1941 the German authorities kept issuing edicts that targeted the Jewish population in the Netherlands. By the end of this year, the Jews had been isolated and removed from society. From work to play to school, Jews were no longer allowed to be part of the activity with non-Jews in the country. As the weeks and months rolled by, the number of children in Shula's class at school dwindled. By 1942, the SS was in full force with its plans of rounding up Jews, putting them into the ghettos they had set up in the major city of Amsterdam, and then sending them off to the Westerbork deportation center in Holland, where they would then be transported primarily to the death camps in Poland, Auschwitz-Birkenau and Sobibor.

Shula's two oldest siblings, Leo and Esther, knew they could not wait much longer. They went to work, looking to find hiding places for their younger sisters and brother. By good fortune, Esther made contact with Corneila (Cok) Ouweleen and Maria Louise (Mies) Hoefsmit.

Cok and Mies were two Christian women who lived in the same house. They worked as teachers at a Jewish vocational school in Amsterdam. In 1942, they lost their jobs at this school as the German authorities announced that non-Jews teaching Jewish children was now strictly forbidden.

While they were able to find work with a Dutch non-Jewish school, these two courageous women did not sit by idly. They became active in helping to hide Jewish children, sometimes in their own home and other times in the homes of other people. Cok and Mies initially took in Esther, Avraham, and Sara and placed Hannah and Shula elsewhere in Amsterdam.

Shula ended up in the apartment of Mrs. Junkman. Leo had arranged forged papers and provided them to the Asscher family, who were initially reluctant to let Shula go. The papers said that Shula had already been deported to Westerbork, which would be important when the SS would come and wonder why the family had one less person around.

Leo did not go into hiding, as he had work to do for his siblings. Now eighteen, he had connected with a Zionist Jewish group that was working to sneak young adult Jews out of Nazi-controlled Europe and into British-controlled Palestine. Leo had made it into Belgium with the particular group he was with and was told one evening to wait at the place at which they stopped until the group's leader returned. Leo and a friend in the group did not wait. Thinking they could run out to get cigarettes and be back quickly, they ventured out against instructions. They were captured by the German authorities. Leo was sent to Sobibor and did not survive the war.

Meanwhile, hidden at Mrs. Junkman's home was four-teen-year-old Shula. One evening in the spring of 1943, she encountered a gentleman named Frans Wijnakker, there to help her get away. With the Nazis having a very tight grip on the major cities in the Netherlands, let alone with many Dutch Nazis and sympathizers lurking around, staying in Amsterdam would be very risky. So this couple-hour train ride with this unknown man to the rural south was Shula's best chance for survival.

Unbeknownst to Frans, sitting nearby Shula on the first leg of the train ride to Den Bosch to look out for her and make sure she made the transfer smoothly to Raven-stein, which was reassuring to Shula, were two middle-aged Dutch teachers: Cok and Mies. Later on in his new work, Frans would meet these two women directly.

Shula, now known as Freetje DeGroot, and Frans would arrive safely to his home in Dieden. She not only would be the first Jew they would take into hiding but would also be the one they would have their greatest feelings over, emo-tions of both fear and care.

Chapter Four:
Life in Occupied
Netherlands

Frans Wijnakker's simple response of yes to a call for help while in Amsterdam now fully thrusted he and Mien into the harsh realities of life in the Netherlands that most of the Dutch population, especially in the cities, was experiencing under the occupation and control of Nazi Germany. After the Netherlands was conquered by Germany in May 1940, the next few months were relatively quiet under German rule. The Germans viewed the Dutch as kindred spirits and thought they would be excited by the Germans coming in and would want to join their empire, the Third Reich—not so for many of the Dutch.

This relative period of tranquility would be short-lived. Before 1940 was over, the German authorities started to force their will on the Dutch. Each year of the occupation, five years in total, would be worst than the year before. Unlike the rest of the German-occupied countries in northern and western Europe that were freed during the fall of 1944, the Netherlands would not be fully liberated until May 5, 1945. (Germany officially surrendered to the Allies on May 7, 1945.)

In the end, oppressive and brutal summarized what this occupation was like for the Dutch under German rule. There were four main areas of emphasis of how the German authorities ran this country for five miserable years.

First emphasis: Control the flow of information, the news that people receive. In the days of the 1940s that was easier to do than in our world of today. Television was coming soon into people's live, but not until after World War II was well done. Internet, what the heck is that? Not a concept that the world of the 1940s could yet imagine.

With radio and newspapers as the primary sources of how people got their news in Holland in the 1940s, Nazi censorship and propaganda could easily take over and control the information Dutch citizens received. Freedom of the press was gone now. Not surprisingly, as the war progressed and resistance efforts from the Dutch picked up, underground newspapers appeared to give the citizenry the real news and truth. Of course, such activity was illegal from publishing these newspapers to reading them. Don't get caught.

In addition, before 1940 was out, the German authorities issued an edict, ordering all the Dutch to not listen to their radios—not an easy order to enforce with a country of nine million people. As the war years moved forward, the German authorities suspected that many people in the Netherlands were disregarding this order. Those who did would start to pick up secret broadcasts coming out of London, England: the BBC, British Broadcasting Corporation, and Radio Orange, the station set up by the Dutch government in exile where even Queen Wilhelmina would come on at times to speak. If one was listening to these secret broadcasts by mid 1943, they would hear the truth about what was happening in the war. The Germans, who were dominating the continent of Europe just a year-and-a-half ago, were now starting to suffer defeat after defeat on the battlefield. The German authorities did not want to give people in the Netherlands any sign of hope. September 1943, Hanns Rauter, the head of the SS, issued a nationwide decree. Owning a radio was now against the law; all Dutch citizens must now turn in their radios. Many of the Dutch went along compliantly with the order, some with their wry Dutch humor turned in broken down radios to comply. The Germans even conducted raids on people's homes to collect radios. Interesting enough, when this order came, Frans hid his radio and never turned it in. Following the rules like everyone else was not his forte.

Second emphasis of how the German authorities ran this country: exploit all resources. The Germans never had enough of their own raw materials, supplies, and parts for all the manufacturing needed to build this huge war machine they had going. So they took the materials they needed from the many countries they occupied in Europe, including the Netherlands. What economic hardships this caused was not their concern.

Included in this taking of materials was food. In particular, cattle became scarce in the Netherlands as the war moved forward. The meat and dairy from cattle helped the Germans feed their soldiers and citizens of the Reich. So when a Frans Wijnakker started showing up in the cities in the west such as Amsterdam and The Hague, selling valuable and somewhat scarce food like meat and eggs, people were willing to pay under the table and engage with him in this black market business. Especially for people in the cities, to get food and other supplies from stores was restricted by German-issued ration cards they were suppose to use. Guilders, the Dutch currency of the time still remained, especially in the illegal and underground economy in which Frans was one of the active participants—along with being a good salesman too.

In addition, in terms of exploiting resources, the Germans also needed people. The Germans suffered a labor shortage during World War II. They did not have enough able-bodied men let alone some women to work the factories and fields to support their huge war machine activity. Where were these people? They were helping Germany fight two wars at once: 1) what we now call the Holocaust where thousands upon thousands were needed to run the hundreds of concentration camps and related operations, and 2) what is now called World War II. Germany had over ten million soldiers fighting for it all over Europe and in North Africa. So how did the Germans make up for this labor shortage? The term for it was called forced labor, meaning you got the assignment to go work in Germany or elsewhere in Europe in the factories and fields for their big war effort. The Germans ordered many people from the countries they occupied to come to work for them, including from its next door neighbor the Netherlands. During the course of the war, 350,000 Dutch citizens went to work in Germany. 30,000 did not come home alive from this forced labor, and some came home disabled. Once the Dutch got wind of what this forced labor was all about, with the unemployed usually being the first targets to go, they were frightened. Going to work in Germany was not a job assignment anyone wanted. Later in the war, Frans would get an order to report for medical evaluation, the preliminary step before going to work in Germany—a major obstacle he would have to overcome.

A third emphasis of how the Germans ran occupied Netherlands: stamp out resistance in any form it showed. Freedom of speech was now gone. If you were heard criticizing the Germans, you could be arrested if not tortured and beaten. Showing displays of Dutch nationalism and admiration for the royalty were outlawed by the German authorities.

In time, the Dutch would rise up with a few major protests and strikes during the course of the war. Don't get involved. The Nazi response was one of much brutality. As example, the first major such outburst was the Workers Strike of late February 1941. Over 100,000 people hit the streets in Amsterdam, and more in a half dozen other cities around the country in the second day of the strike, protesting the oppressive rule of the Germans and the first roundup of Jews out of Amsterdam to concentration camps. The German authorities were extremely upset at this awful disturbance. Force, arrest, and execution—a common pattern they would show—were the response.

Nine people were killed when soldiers fired into a crowd of protesters, and the so-called ringleaders, nearly 20, would be arrested and later put on trial and executed.

Even more brutal was the Nazi authorities response to the Milk Strike that occurred in late April 1943. The Germans were now seeking former Dutch soldiers for forced labor in Germany. Farmers who deliver milk were ready to stop this service in protest, with the initial protest beginning with workers at a milk factory in eastern Netherlands. After the first day of the strike, the Nazi authorities had executed 80 of these workers from the factory, putting up their pictures as posters to serve as a deterrence. The strike was over after three days, with another 95 people shot to death and 400 wounded.

The last winter of the war, which people in Holland refer to as the Hunger Winter, was sparked by the last major strike during this period.

It was from the railway workers, who had spent the war helping the Germans by shipping out materials to Germany and people to the concentration camps. With urging from the Dutch government in exile, the railway workers walked off the job in September 1944—with most going into hiding. The bulk of the German personnel occupying the country were in the major cities of the west, where over one-third of the population resided. The response from the German authorities can be summed up as, "Too bad Dutch people, we'll take care of what we need. Fend for yourself." The Germans let the Dutch trains sit by idly, and used trucks and their own trains to ship in the food and supplies they needed to care for their personnel.

As winter 1945 rolled around, food supplies in the western part of the country dwindled. People started to eat tulips to survive. Those who could went on scavenger hunts to other parts of the country to try and get food. The Dutch government in exile pleaded with the Allied forces to help. But airlifts of food from the Allies came in too little too late to help much. The Allies were now preoccupied with marching in to Germany to defeat Hitler and not wanting to risk greatly having their planes shot down over Holland. This Hunger Winter in the end saw 20,000 Dutch citizens starve to death.

By the middle of the war, 1943, a half dozen main resistance organizations were now operating by the Dutch. They were involved in such risky and dangerous activities as forging false identity papers, running underground newspapers, espionage, sabotage, and hit-and-run attacks against Dutch Nazi collaborators and on occasion, even the Germans. As with protests and strikes, if one of these attacks hit the Dutch Nazis or any German personnel, the response was one of brutal reprisal. For instance, in February 1943 one of the high ranking Dutch Nazis helping the Germans in their occupation of the Netherlands, General Hendrik Seyffardt, was stationed in the capital city of The Hague. One evening his doorbell rang and two resistance fighters from the Communist group shot him dead. When Hanns Rauter got wind of this, he ordered fifty Dutch people currently housed in jails to be rounded up and executed. Later in 1943 Operation Silbertanne got rolling. It was the code name of a secret murder squad consisting of Dutch Nazis. They assassinated over 50 Dutch citizens over the course of a year.

The Germans were big on setting examples. In October 1944, when Dutch resistance fighters killed a German SS intelligence officer, in reprisal, the Germans rounded up 29 people in the Apollolaan neighborhood of Amsterdam and had them publicly executed, with neighbors pulled in to watch.

So as Dutch resistance organizations picked up their activity in 1943 so too did the reign of terror imposed by the German authorities on the Dutch population, which did not let up until the country was fully liberated in May 1945.

These resistance groups in the Netherlands faced some major obstacles in trying to combat the Germans. One was terrain. In other parts of Europe, resistance fighters could attack and then wade into deep forest ranges or up in the mountains, making it difficult for the Germans to find them. The Netherlands is a relatively flat country with some trees but no deep forests. Lots of water in the country. So if you could hold your breath under water a long time, you would do just fine in the resistance.

In addition, the Dutch resistance groups operated independently from one another for most of the war. None of them ever had the firepower and manpower to match the Germans. During the occupation, nearly 20,000 members of various Dutch resistance groups got arrested and jailed, with some sent off to concentration camps or into forced labor. 2,000 got executed for their risky work.

Of all the resistance groups in the Netherlands, the one that would become the largest and most effective was known by its initials L.O. Full name in Dutch: Landelijke Organsatsie voor Hulpen Underduikers. English translation: The National Organization for Helping People in Hiding. During the course of the war the L.O. would help hide over 300,000 people from the German authorities. Quite effective.

But this work was very risky and dangerous. Helena Kuipers Reitberg, Tante (Aunt) Riek as she was affectionately known, was one of the founders and leaders of the L.O. Later in the war, she would get betrayed and captured by the Germans and sent off to the Ravensbruck concentration camp in Germany, where she would die before the war's end.

By the time the L.O. was well established with a network of helpers around the country, it was mid 1943. Too late to help many of the Jews.

Approximately 25,000 Jews made it into hiding. But since Jews were the number one target, over one-third of them got captured and then deported to the concentration camps. So of those non-Jews willing to get involved in this dangerous work of helping hide people from the German authorities, far more were helping hide non-Jews rather than Jews.

For those Dutch who played an active role in any of the resistance groups, they often had to worry more about their fellow Dutch citizens than just the German personnel occupying their country. In the 1930s various fascist or Nazi-type political parties sprang into existence throughout much of Europe, the United States too, and in the Netherlands as well. Known by its initials, the N.S.B., the Nationaal Socialistische Beweging (National Socialist Movement) was the Dutch Nazi party started in 1931 by Anton Mussert. Prior to the war the N.S.B. was not large in number, and the Dutch who generally are politically moderate mostly ignored the N.S.B.'ers as extremist idiots. Within a year after Germany's occupation of the Netherlands was in full force, a good 100,000 people had signed up and joined the N.S.B. How come? They wanted to be on the winning team. By the end of 1941 Germany was not only dominating their country but nearly all of Europe.

The Germans needed help in keeping the government of the Netherlands running. When existing managers within the civil service were not too enthused to be working for the Nazi authorities, they were excused from their jobs and replaced by loyal N.S.B.'ers. Being part of the N.S.B. meant not only the opportunity for good jobs but also a much less of a life of restrictions imposed on the rest of the Dutch population. N.S.B.'ers got to keep their radios, they ate better, and they did not have to worry about getting their bicycles confiscated, or hauled off into forced labor. And when the Nazis deported people off to the concentration camps, they looted their belongings with some of the helpful N.S.B.'ers getting to have some of this bounty.

In addition, some people just to stay on the good side of the Nazi authorities helped them out by doing their jobs and complying with the requests from the Nazis: university administrators helping expel Jewish professors and students, civil service employees keeping records on the population, police officers going along in raids to round up targets for deportation as example. Some young Dutch women provided sexual company to the German police and soldiers, who looked so good in their uniforms.

Whether one was sympathetic to the Germans or just going along by following orders, a person could make extra money in these hard economic times just by acting on suspicions. The Germans paid cash bounties to people who reported suspicious activity to them, especially centered around those who were hiding people the Germans were after—the Jews being the top target on that list. One group, in particular, specialized in this. It was known as the Henneicke Column. A man named Wim Henneicke started this unit, a group of bounty hunters. In 1943 at the height of the deportation of Jews from the Netherlands, and thus Jews seeking to get into hiding, this band of bounty hunters was able to track down and have captured over 8,000 Jews.

So between the N.S.B.'ers, sympathizers, and compliant helpers with the German authorities, those Dutch involved in the various core resistant groups were outnumbered by their fellow Dutch who posed a great threat to them and made life easier for the Germans.

As mentioned at the start of this chapter, the Germans had four main areas of emphasis in how they ran the occupied country of Holland. Three have been covered. The fourth area of emphasis was their number one priority: persecute, isolate, and deport the entire Jewish population they could get their hands on. Prior to the occupation, the

Jewish population in the Netherlands was just over one-and-a-half percent of the total population.

The Nazi policy to rid the country of its Jews, never announced to the general public, started out slowly. Before 1940 ended, the early edicts targeting Jews began. For instance, Jews who worked in civil service jobs and in university positions such as professors were fired from these jobs because they were Jews. At this point in the history of Jewish life in the Netherlands, only handful of Jews had achieved these positions of importance. Among them and affected by this early edict was a man named Lodewijk Visser, the most prominent Jew in the country. He was the head of the Dutch High Court, an equivalent role to Chief Justice of the U.S. Supreme Court. His dismissal was met with silence from his fellow justices and most everyone else of importance among the Dutch government and society.

The German authorities were quite pleased by this response or lack thereof by the Dutch. It was the green light for them to go ahead and continue the persecution of the Jewish people. As mentioned in the previous chapter, the edicts against Jews continued throughout all of 1941 so that by the end of the year the Jewish population had been isolated and removed from the non-Jewish population. For instance, going to school with non-Jews, can't do. Working with non-Jews, can't do. Attending university, Jews are not allowed. Own your own business, taken away. Go out and enjoy social and recreational activities like anyone else, Jews are now prohibited. In January 1942, the shift of people was on. The forty percent of the Jewish population who lived in other parts of the country outside the major city of Amsterdam were moved into the city and put into three districts set up as ghettos. By May 1942 when Jews went out into public, the yellow Star of David or the badge of humiliation that identified a person as a Jew, had to be visible on their clothes.

By July 1942 the trains were cranking. The Jewish population now bunched into Amsterdam were being lined up bit by bit at the Hollandse Schouwberg, the Dutch Theater, and shipped via transit centers like Camp Westerbork and Camp Vucht in the Netherlands primarily to the death camps in Poland, Auschwitz-Birkenau and Sobibor. By the end of September 1943, the entire Jewish population the Nazis could get their hands on, with help from the Dutch locals, had been deported.

Many Jews let alone non-Jews had no idea what was happening. The Nazi propaganda was active, with messages telling the whole population of Holland that the Jews were being sent to work camps in Germany to help out. False.

For those Jews who sensed doom was coming, their best hope was to go into hiding.

But to do that, help would be needed. Would anyone help?

Contrary to popular belief about the Dutch, the answer to this question was not many. While the violent anti-Semitism seen in much of Eastern and Central Europe was not prevelant in Holland, for the vast majority of Dutch in the 1940s indifference, fear of Nazi reprisals, and just trying to survive the economic hardships and restrictive rule of the Germans was enough to occupy their lives. Even those Dutch willing to take the dangerous risk of involvement in a core resistant group, outside of the L.O., most did not pay heed to the plight of their fellow Jews. Again, they had enough to worry about with the German authorities and all the N.S.B.'ers and other Dutch sympathizers with the Germans.

So this was the world of the Netherlands that Frans Wijnakker with the support of his wife Mien plunged themselves into by answering yes to a call for help to take a young Jewish girl home for three weeks. It was a world most people in the Netherlands and other occupied countries under the wrath of Nazi Germany stayed far away from and never entered.

Chapter Five:
The New Business
Starts Expanding

This new guest, Freetje, spent her time playing outside with the four young children of the Wijnakker family. She also helped Mien in the kitchen, doing the dishes, clearing the table, getting the food out for meals. Mien was teaching her how to take care of a home.

After having Freetje for a week, one day, Mien asked Frans, "Where does this child come from? Do you know where her parents are?"

"I don't know either," Frans answered. "I picked her up from a lady in Amsterdam."

"You know, Frans, I think she is a Jewish girl."

"Yes, that's right."

"Did you know?"

"Yes," he said, "and I brought her anyway. They are really poor souls."

As the days moved forward, Freetje started to open up and talk more with Mien. Mien learned that Freetje was born in Germany and was one of six children in her family, all of whom escaped Germany and had been hidden. Her older brother had joined up with a group that would hopefully get him to Palestine. They had all been received and living in Amsterdam before having to go into hiding. Back at home in Germany, her parents had a store. Everything was destroyed in November 1938, and her parents essentially lost everything. They brought their children to the Dutch border a short time after that. Freetje did not know now how her parents were doing.

Mien quickly became attached to Freetje, who let Mien know she wanted very much to stay with the Wijnakker family if that was possible. Mien wanted this to happen too and had discussions with Frans about letting Freetje stay beyond a few weeks with them.

Mien continued her discussions with Frans, wanting to do more. She said to him assertively, "Freetje has a younger brother who is hiding in Amsterdam. When you go there again, you can bring him back with you. Then she will have companionship. She longs for that. Please go get him."

Frans agreed and acted on the contact information that Freetje provided him. Approximately a couple of weeks after Freetje's arrival, Frans brought home Avraham out of Amsterdam in the dark just like he had done the first time with Freetje. Avraham was a couple of years younger than his sister Shula (now called Freetje), but he looked younger and was small in stature too. So Frans thought he was less than ten years old. Avraham was given the Dutch name Fritsje. One of the soldiers who had been quartered with the Wijnakkers was named Frits Slinger. He had a child somewhere between seven and nine years old. So the story agreed to was that if something went wrong, Fritsje would be the son of Frits Slinger out here visiting on vacation in Dieden.

Not too long after the arrival of Freetje and Fritsje came Agnes. Her real name was Suzie Klazer. Upon moving in to the Wijnakker household, she was called Agnes Loohuis. Loohuis was the last name of a soldier who was quartered with the Wijnakkers a few years back.

In 1943, Agnes was seventeen years old and was actually still a child herself. She had served as an aid in a nursery in a building in Amsterdam. At this place were Jewish children separated from their parents who were in another part of the same building. Many of the parents had already been transported away by the Nazis. If Agnes had stayed, she would eventually have been transported away with the children. While she was very attached to the children and really did not want to desert them, she eventually made the tough choice to leave, due especially to the urging by a pair of Dutch teachers (Cok and Mies) who bravely volunteered to help care for the Jewish children. Cok and Mies would help bring Agnes out of Amsterdam to the Wijnakker home. That proved to be quite a challenge. More on that coming in the next chapter.

What this meant now is that Frans and Mien had three Jewish children refugees under their care and in their home along with their four small children. Did they recognize what they had gotten into with all its implications and potential dangers? Probably not fully yet. But they proceeded because they were just trying to be helpful.

✻

Sara, a younger sister of Freetje and Fritsje, came a little later. Thanks to those two former teachers from Amsterdam, Cok and Mies as they were known, Sara was brought out on the train to the Wijnakker home and stayed for a short time. She later was moved around and stayed with various families throughout the southern part of Holland in order to be kept safe.

She started in Haren and spent much of her time in Ravenstein, able to maintain some contact with her brother and sister. In fact, Fritsje was placed with Frans's mother for a while before later returning to stay put in the home of Frans and Mien. Such a practice by Frans, serving as a broker to find safe refuge for Jews, would expand in the fall of 1943 and actively continue throughout 1944. His home could only hide a few Jewish refugees. At its height, the Wijnakkers often would have eight extra residents, Jewish refugees, in their home and at times up to ten.

Chapter Six:
Early Challenges
and Dangers

As the business of hiding and finding refuge for Jews picked up in 1943, so too did the risk involved. One such challenge occurred with the arrival of Agnes.

Two ladies heard about Frans Wijnakker through a pre-war acquaintance of his. As mentioned in Chapter Three, it was Cok and Mies, who had helped Shula (or Freetje) and her siblings along with other Jewish children they used to teach, although Frans never knew these ladies' names or where they came from. They were the ones who also picked up Agnes in Amsterdam and brought her to Dieden by train. The trip there went off without problems. The return trip for the two ladies went, initially, less well.

With wartime and the restrictions imposed from the Nazi Germany occupation on the people of the Netherlands, unless one had an official permit, the trading and transporting of food was prohibited. For guiding Agnes to

Dieden, Frans provided the two women eggs, which they gladly accepted and packed inside their suitcases to hide.

Cok and Mies then went on their way to the train station in Ravenstein to return to Amsterdam. Frans took Freetje on the back of his bicycle and accompanied the ladies. They traveled on the lane behind the convent that was up high above the Maas River.

When they arrived at the railway station, standing there was the police chief of Ravenstein, Chief van Meul, along with one of his officers. Frans did not trust the police chief. Some of the policemen in the area of Dieden knew that Frans was involved in something, and Frans was worried what this chief would do if he knew what that something was.

Frans had had a run-in with Chief van Meul a couple years before. Earlier in the war, owning a radio was not illegal yet but listening to it was. In this prior incident, several people were visiting at Fran's house and were listening to the radio. When Chief van Meul arrived there, they became scared. At first, Frans did not know what to do about the situation, as the chief stood at his front door with a stern look on his face while the radio was playing. But then Frans challenged the chief, saying that he had heard that the police chief went around to people's houses to see if they were listening to a radio—in essence, acting like a spy on his own people. Frans proceeded to tell the chief he had heard everywhere that Chief van Meul had a bad reputation as a result.

The police chief stood silently for a moment and then left, probably because of this daring challenge made by Frans.

Now, with Chief van Meul standing at the train station, Frans did not say anything to him or even look his way. He said farewell to the women and left with Freetje to bicycle back to Dieden. The chief then ordered the policeman with him to get on his bicycle and follow Frans.

A short distance later after leaving the town square of Ravenstein, Frans stopped and called to the officer, "You're not really following me, are you?"

"Yes, I've been ordered to do so," the policeman replied. He knew that Frans had Jews hidden at his house. He looked at the child and said to Frans, "Go home quickly. That would be best."

In the meantime, Chief van Meul had held up Cok and Mies at the train station. He had become suspicious because the two women were not locals he knew and, judging by their dress, were likely from one of the cities. So he wondered why they would be in this small-town area.

He commanded them to open their luggage. In searching their belongings, he found the eggs packed under their clothes. He then ordered them to come with him to the police station.

At the police station, in an interrogating tone, Chief van Meul barked at the two women, "Where did you get these eggs?"

Neither one answered. They sat silently as he tried asking again. He then locked them up in a cell and left the station.

A short time after arriving home, one of the local people from town came to tell Frans what had happened, that the two ladies he had been with had been arrested for hiding eggs.

Frans then turned around and went back to Ravenstein. Initially he thought of going straight to the police chief's house and verbally challenging him to stop with this nonsense over a few eggs. Instead, he went directly to the police station. No one was there, and the station was locked up. So he climbed over the fence to go to the back of the station where the cells were. A neighbor saw and called out, "I'll tell! I'll tell the chief that you came to the door!"

Frans ignored the neighbor and continued walking as if nothing was happening. When he came to the back of the station, he called to the two ladies and stated the following instruction, "Say that you exchanged the eggs for a small electric pan."

A short time later Frans arrived back home. Waiting there was none other than Chief van Meul, who asked, "Where are you coming from?"

"Me? From the village," Frans replied.

"Where have you been?"

"I was visiting Van Boxtel," Frans explained, although he had not been at this friend's house in Ravenstein.

"We have two ladies at the police station. Did they buy eggs from you?"

"Not buy, but we did an exchange for a small electric pan," Frans explained.

"Where did these ladies come from? They are strange. They don't say anything. You seem to be the obvious person these days who has contact with such strange types of people."

"Oh?" Frans said in a somewhat irritated tone.

"But exchanging goods is also not allowed. Where did you get those eggs?" Chief van Meul asked in a demanding tone.

"I got them from Janske and from De Looier." These were two local farmers.

The chief continued with his interrogation of Frans. "And how much did you pay for them?"

"Twelve and a half cents."

The chief, with a puzzled look on his face, then said, "That is cheap. They are much more expensive than that."

After this exchange, Frans talked the chief into going back to the police station so they could all talk with the ladies and put this matter to rest. At the station, Chief van Meul brought the ladies out from the cell. They told the chief that they had traded an electric pan for the eggs. They were then set free.

As they departed for the train station, they got a warning against antisocial behavior and were not allowed to take the eggs. Chief van Meul then gave Frans a warning, "I will have order. Nothing happens in this community without me knowing it. Keep that in mind!"

This would not be the last time Chief van Meul would pose a challenge to Frans in his endeavors.

(Of special note, Cornelia Ouweleen and Maria Louise Hoefsmit—Cok and Mies, respectively—were recognized by Yad Vashem in 1968 as Righteous Among the Nations for their courageous actions to help save and hide Jewish children. Later in the war, they also helped hide young Dutch men to protect them from being conscripted in the German army.)

＊

As life continued in the summer of 1943, Frans and Mien now had three Jewish children under their care. They all operated under Dutch names: Freetje, Fritsje, and Agnes. Because the three children had dark hair that gave them that Jewish appearance, Frans and Mien decided to bleach their hair to give them a lighter color and help make them look more like Dutch children. On one of his trips to Amsterdam, Frans bought and brought home water peroxide, a substance best known for removing ink spots. It was used to bleach the Jewish children's hair, changing the color from black to white. This so-called bleach initially burned and blistered their scalps. After a few weeks, especially for Freetje and Agnes, it started to fade and eventually their light-colored hair returned to its darkened state.

Freetje, in particular, was most around. After a short while at the Wijnakkers' home, Fritsje was most often staying at the home of Frans's mother in Haren, and Agnes was often out working, doing housekeeping for others in their homes.

Freetje would sometimes accompany Frans on his errands. As she would be out and about in the community, the story told was she was an orphan whose parents died in the bombing that hit Rotterdam. She even attended church with the Wijnakker family.

But after being with the Wijnakkers for a few months, fear hit one day. A neighbor in Dieden came to Frans one day and said that he thought that Freetje was a Jewish girl. Neighbors had been talking since they certainly saw

Freetje out in the community, sometimes accompanying Frans.

Frans said little in response. He went home and shared this encounter with Mien. They became afraid of getting discovered. So Frans then talked to Freetje. He told her that she was now, at age fifteen, quite capable of working and taking care of herself. Maybe it would be best for her to go away for a little while until this gossip and attention died down. He provided her a bicycle to help. So that next day Freetje rode away, saying good-bye to the townspeople as they were on their way to church.

Freetje rode on her bicycle to a nearby village and came upon a fairly good-sized farm. She knocked on the door of the home there and asked the farmer if she could work for him in exchange for room and board. She was taken in and put to work, helping to clean the house as well as learning to milk the cows and do chores on the farm. After ten days living and working here, the farmer asked her one day if she was Jewish, since that was the word he was hearing from others in the village. She said yes and left quietly the next morning.

Freetje then rode to another local village and was able to find another farm to stay on and work. But after a week or so there, the same question came up again, with her riding away quietly the next day. This pattern continued a couple of more times until a very tired and scared Freetje rode to the Wijnakker home one night, knocking on the door at two o'clock in the morning.

Frans and Mien were both awakened and expressed delight at seeing Freetje at their door. They welcomed her into the house.

A tired Freetje asked, "Can I stay here and not leave any more?"

Mien nodded her head, and Frans said, "Yes, you are most welcome to stay here. Probably best that you stay in the house and not go out in town any more."

Freetje nodded her head in agreement, and Frans and Mien both smiled, happy to see her again.

Many years later as Frans, a few years before his death, told the stories about his experience during the war, he spoke about the incident of sending Freetje away as one he and Mien most regretted. He would tell the incident as occurring later on in 1944 rather than 1943 and due to the house overflowing with refugees. Since Freetje was now a little older, the thinking was she could be ready to be placed elsewhere. So a new place was arranged for her in Groningen, a city a few hours away in the northern part of the Netherlands. A teacher there would take her in. But when that woman got frightened a short time later at the danger of taking in a Jewish girl, Freetje found her way to the train and returned back to the Wijnakkers in Dieden.

As Freetje herself reported some years later, when sent away, she never left the local area around Ravenstein and Dieden in the south. For Frans, this regret involving Freetje turned out well in the end. She remained with the Wijnakker family until the end of the war. Mien would always view her fondly, and Freetje often helped teach manners to the four young Wijnakker children. Frans would not back away again from further challenges and risks he faced in helping find refuge for Jews during World War II.

Meanwhile, around that same time during the late summer of 1943, Freetje's brother Fritsje encountered a scare while in Haren. One day Fritsje was out riding his bicycle around the area. He used the name of Frits Slinger when he went out of the house, with his head of white hair as part of his new persona. He saw something burning coming from Haren and then, out of curiosity, rode his bicycle closer to see what was going on. One of the residents of Haren, a neighbor of Frans's mother, came up to Fritsje and asked, "Who are you?"

"I am Frits Slinger. I saw something burning and thought it must be a fire," Fritsje replied.

The neighbor, with a look of doubt on his face, then said, "I think that you are a Jew and not Slinger."

Fritsje said nothing in return. He turned around and rode his bicycle all the way to the Wijnakker house in Dieden. He did not dare go to Haren again to stay with Frans's mother. Frans and Mien then thought it best that Fritsje and Freetje stay at home so they would not be seen in public again.

When someone would come to the house unexpectedly, the fear of a house search would hit, and the children would suddenly flee the house and hide themselves in the fields. There wasn't a good hiding place in the Wijnakker house. With an ever suspicious Chief van Meul nearby, the threat of a raid on the house grew.

Beyond the Ravenstein police chief, another person of the local area who would be a thorn to Frans was the parish priest, Father Johannes Simons. Frans had engaged in occasional conversations with the priest about his business of trading meat and eggs. The priest had laughed when told about the butchering of cattle and the trade in meat and eggs. The way the priest would ask questions, though, sometimes came across more as prying to check out the talk he heard from others than showing curiosity and interest about the work of one of his parishioners.

Then one day in 1943, Father Simons confronted Frans and was not laughing at all. The priest had heard something from his circle of clergymen within the parish community as well as from the curate, or head, of the whole parish, who was located in the nearby town of Berghem. When he saw Frans bicycling by in Ravenstein this day, Father Simons called to him.

When Frans stopped by the gate where the clergyman was standing, the priest began. "Come here, close to me. I heard something terrible."

"About me?" Frans asked.

"Yes. If it is really true, it is terrible," the priest responded.

"What did you hear?"

"While I was recently visiting the curate in Berghem, a young man came to us and said to me that I have someone in my church that I should greatly admire. When I asked who deserves such admiration, not something I would readily do anyway, he tells me it's you, Frans Wijnakker. And when I ask why, he tells me it's because you are hiding Jewish children in your house."

The priest continued. "I couldn't believe what I heard. I have to know what happens in my parish. If this is true, it is so dangerous. And now I ask you, it is surely not true?"

The parish priest was viewed as a man of great authority, not someone to whom one would lie. "Yes," Frans answered calmly, "it is true. I have Jewish children in my home."

The priest sighed deeply and then exclaimed, "Wijnakker, what have you done! Why are you involved in this? Send these children away as soon as possible. Where did you get them?"

"I can't send them away. I have them, and they are not leaving," Frans boldly responded.

"Can't you get rid of them?" Father Simons asked.

"No, I can't get rid of them. We are doing it because otherwise they will all be killed."

"Who says that?" the priest asked incredulously.

"I know what will happen," Frans matter-of-factly stated. "Hitler and his Nazis are shipping Jews, including children, to their camps to have them killed."

The Catholic clergyman argued back. "A head of state would never do that, kill children. I don't believe a word of it. They also have responsibilities. I don't believe a word of it. These children have to work. They would have to go to a camp, but they would have to work. And what would happen to the children? They would go to school there. They have schools there. No, Wijnakker, killing is not true. A head of state would never do that."

Father Simons continued, "I don't understand you at all. What were you thinking?"

"But they are also human beings," Frans responded.

The priest shot back, "They are Jews. What are you involved in? They are Jews!"

"That they are. But they are human beings too." Frans even gave a friendly smile to the pastor.

"Well, yes," the priest said. "But they are Jews. They hung our dear LORD on the cross, and you take them in your home!"

"But these Jews did not do that, Father. These are children."

Father Simons walked away shaking his head. It would not be the last time he presented a challenge to Frans and the aid he was trying to provide.

✳

Challenges occurred for Agnes too. The shift of her life from Amsterdam to Dieden was an enormous change. She had gone from a well-ordered, polished city life to one of raw country living with different concepts of cleanliness, hygiene, and speech. She had to adapt, as there was no choice.

Agnes helped Mien with the housekeeping, and later she helped Mien's mother, who lived in Haren. There were still three older children at home, younger siblings of Mien who were not yet married. Frans and Mien had instructed Agnes not to tell Mien's mother and siblings that she was Jewish. Mien's mother was considered a big gossip, so they did not want to take a chance. The line was that she was Agnes Loohuis who had come from Amsterdam.

In Haren lived someone who was thought to be a German sympathizer. Agnes heard that and became afraid. She told Frans so one day after returning from a day of work as the housekeeper for Mien's mother.

Upon hearing the concern that Agnes expressed, Frans replied, "You are just being foolish. This man is not a member of the NSB. You don't have to be scared because no one knows you are Jewish. If you bike there and back every day, no one will suspect anything. You are just here in the area to recover and regain your health."

Yet a short time later, one of Mien's younger brothers, Bertus, who lived at home with Mien's mother in Haren, said to Agnes when she was working in the house, "You are really a Jewess, aren't you?"

Upon hearing about this interaction that evening from Agnes, Frans and Mien decided that when Agnes went to Haren the next day it would be for the last time. The story they went with was that Agnes had received a telegram asking her to come home immediately to Amsterdam because her mother was ill. Mien's mother could then tell everyone that her help went home. They would not think that her help was Jewish, and the illness story would be spread about. After that, Agnes did not go to Haren again.

One Sunday, a short time later, Frans and Mien did something that almost never happened: they went to church together. With four young children at home, going out together for any occasion did not happen often at all. They had told Agnes to clean up a little and not to allow in anyone. What Bertus, Mien's brother, almost never did, he did. He came to visit. All the doors of the house were locked. But a window was unlocked from the inside, and through pushing that up, he climbed in and entered the Wijnakker house.

Agnes had not noticed, as she was busy cleaning. When Agnes entered the front room, Bertus saw her.

"I thought that you were in Amsterdam," he said to her.

"Yes, I was, but I came back last night," said a startled but quick-thinking Agnes.

"Are you staying long?"

"No, I have to go back tomorrow because my mother is still sick."

Mien had this feeling of worry while sitting in church. She told Frans, and they both left the church early. To their great amazement, when they returned home, they saw her brother sitting inside.

"I thought she had left," Bertus said to Frans and Mien while pointing at Agnes.

"Yes, you are right. She is leaving again," Frans quickly replied.

"But I know anyway that she is Jewish," Bertus boldly stated.

Frans then said, "Listen. Do not tell that to anyone. It is much too dangerous if the Germans get wind of this. And besides, if the Underground hears about you doing that, they may shoot you dead."

Mien went one step further. She sternly said to her brother, "If you open your mouth, I'll shoot you myself!"

"No, no, I won't tell anybody," her shaken brother responded. Bertus departed back to Haren shortly afterward.

Chapter Seven:
The Pivotal Moment
and Forging
a Key Ally

Frans Wijnakker continued his usual business of trading in meat and eggs, even after he took three Jewish children into his home and kept an eye on another one, Sara, living nearby with an acquaintance. Then one day in the late summer of 1943 came the pivotal moment in the rescue activities of the Wijnakkers.

A man he did not know came to Fran's house in Dieden for a visit. The man started to ask about buying eggs because he had seen chickens walking around on the Wijnakker property. The stranger called himself Long John, certainly not his real name. From a few questions and comments he made, this stranger seemed to know that Frans had Jewish children hidden in his house, even saying to Frans at one point, "Don't act like it isn't so." Frans grew nervous. Was this man a spy or worse, a police detective coming to arrest me, he wondered to himself.

Then this Long John fellow said this, "You could be of help to us." Who is this guy, Frans wondered even more.

Long John was a key officer with the L.O., the resistance group that helped hide people from the German authorities. Likely the doctor acquaintance in Amsterdam who enlisted Frans to take Freetje out of the city, was also part of the L.O. Frans Wijnakker, after all, seemed to be someone who wanted to help and living in the countryside was a good location for this rescue help. So why not try to get more help from him.

As Long John started to explain the purpose of his visit, Mien had come up and joined in the conversation.

At first, Long John explained simply that he was part of the Dutch Underground. At this point, Frans started to worry a little less.

"What do you do for a living?" he asked of Frans.

"I am actually a miller and am still employed by the Meuleman's granary in Ravenstein. If I have extra time or a day off, I travel to Amsterdam once in a while. I sell things there. When I have the chance, I slaughter a cow. Once a week I sell the meat to the families in the nearby town of Megen. With the fat and also eggs I have, I go to Amsterdam occasionally to sell them there." That he also took meat to Amsterdam, Frans did not want to let on just yet.

Then Long John started to explain further, in a somewhat softer voice. "We're trying to get the remaining Jews still hiding in the cities out before it's too late. You can help us beautifully. You have a large house, but certainly you can't fit everyone that needs help in to your own home."

He continued, "So here's what I would like you to do, if you're willing. My organization can provide you funding to go around the local towns and recruit people to take someone in their home, and to stay in their home, and then you can pay them for it. In essence, you would serve as our point of contact in this area for transporting and placing Jewish refugees. Now I don't want to kid you. This work can be risky and it can be dangerous."

Then Long John looked directly into the eyes of both Frans and Mien and asked simply, "So would you be willing to help?"

Frans and Mien did not need much time to consider. They looked at each other and without hesitation, said together, "We will help."

Long John nodded and smiled. "Listen," he said, "you already have children hiding in your house. If you take your food stuff to sell in Amsterdam and other cities, you are taking a major risk. If the Nazis arrest you, they will come back here and search your house, and then they will find the children. In that case, you and your family will also be in a lot of danger. Therefore, your selling has to stop. You will receive compensation for those that are here and those that will be coming."

Frans spoke up then, "These children we currently have do not have money, as you likely know. A couple come from Germany."

Long John went further. "We will take care that you have enough. You will receive ten guilders per child and fifteen per adult for maintenance, whether they are poor or rich. After the war, no one should be able to say that people earned a lot of money by doing this." Frans took that point very seriously.

Thus the forging of a new and important relationship had begun for Frans. While he did not talk about himself as being a member of the Underground, he would occasionally call upon it for guidance and direction, especially through Long John. Frans had now become the contact for the L.O. and would become a focal point for it in the south, in the province of Brabant, for helping to save Jews in need of hiding. What started from a simple call for help with one Jewish girl would soon escalate into a major rescue operation.

A little time later after his initial visit with Long John, Frans would forge another important relationship that would help him in his new business endeavor. At different times in Dieden, across from the Wijnakker house, grain would be gathered from the fields. When this happened, Frans saw that a gentleman was usually there on hand. His name was Cor van Doorn.

Van Doorn came from Ravenstein. He was a tall, lean man who offered a friendly and warm handshake. He was an official in the Food Provisioning Service. He was doing his job as controller of the food, determining the tax on crops produced by the farmers. On this particular day, Frans went over to take a look at the fieldwork going on and started talking with van Doorn. Van Doorn knew that Frans was known for dealing in meat and eggs. Cor shook hands with Frans and asked, "How's it going, Wijnakker? Still able to earn some money to live on?"

"Yes, it's going okay," Frans answered.

"I haven't heard anything from England in a few weeks. I turned in my radio as we were ordered, so I hear nothing any more about the war."

"I think it is going well," Frans stated.

"How do you know?"

"I have a radio, so I know it firsthand."

"Oh, I would like to listen so much," Cor whispered.

"Are you here this afternoon?" Frans asked.

"Yes, I am here every day," responded Cor.

Then Frans made his bold invitation, speaking up softly to say, "Then come over today at about two to listen. The radio is hidden, but you can understand that. I trust you. You are a van Doorn, a just man. I hear that everywhere."

Owning a radio was now strictly forbidden. As mentioned in Chapter Four, by mid 1943, Germany was now losing the upper hand in the war. Broadcasts from London through the BBC and Radio Orange, kept the Dutch apprised about what was really happening in the war. In fact, speeches throughout the war from Queen Wilhelmina were considered a big morale boost for the citizens of Holland stuck under Nazi rule.

Thus, with the blessing of the ruling governor Arthur Seyss-Inquart, Hanns Rauter, the Nazi head of SS operations in Holland, ordered all radios to be turned in to the authorities in September 1943. To keep these resistant Dutch under control, Rauter realized the Germans must control the flow of information people received and let the Nazi propaganda rule the day.

So unlike many of his compatriots, Frans ignored the edict and kept his radio hidden. This would be a secret kept between Frans and Mien. The radio was hidden in the hayloft above the pigpens in the barn. Via a small hatch, one could turn it on and off. Frans and Cor were listening together when Mien entered the barn.

She got a shock, seeing a strange man in there, as she did not yet know Mr. van Doorn.

In a worried voice, Mien said, "But, Frans, we decided that you would never let anyone else listen to our radio."

"But I know this man," responded Frans.

"Ma'am, don't worry. I am Cor van Doorn. I also have something you are not supposed to have. I have homing pigeons. They are hidden in my house. So we are in the same boat."

"Mien," said Frans, "it's all right. He is a trustworthy man."

"You can say that now. But next there will be someone else who also wants to listen."

"No, no, this is the only man who can listen here," Frans stated emphatically. Mien, still showing a slight worry on her face, then turned around and went back into the house. Frans would assure her more later on about Cor van Doorn.

Cor van Doorn listened to the radio for a short time more with Frans and then was ready to leave.

"Do you have time to come inside for a bit? We can drink a cup of coffee," Frans asked.

"Yes. That would be fine," Cor responded.

Once seated inside the house, Frans opened up to van Doorn. "I've often thought about talking with you, and now I have the chance. You are a civil servant, and you have to do your duty."

"Yes, and?"

"When you were still in the barn, you looked at the window, and there stood a dark girl. She disappeared immediately, but you saw her, did you not?" Frans inquired.

"Yes, I saw her. But that doesn't mean anything," Cor stated.

"Listen," Frans said. "I will let you see the children I have in this house. You can know my secret. No one else must know. I can trust you one hundred percent, right?"

Frans needed someone with whom he could talk and could trust completely. He believed van Doorn was that person. He knew the family as good trustworthy people. Cor's father was a well-respected teacher.

"Van Doorn, you may think I am still a trader. But I don't deal any more. I don't buy or sell anything. I am doing something completely different. It's very serious. No one can know about it. I'll let you see directly."

Frans took van Doorn through the hall to the front room. There were a couple of dark-haired children there, Freetje and Fritsje.

"Are they Jews?" Cor asked.

"Yes, they are Jewish children. I know you distribute food. Maybe you could help me. Would you help?" Frans asked.

"With what?"

"I don't get food coupons. When I visit a farmer, he thinks I am still in the business to buy and sell meat and eggs. But that's no longer the case, but I still have a family and others to feed."

Van Doorn understood Fran's situation and raised his hand to indicate no more explanation was needed. He agreed to help, saying in a reassuring manner, "I'd be happy to help you."

From that moment on, he was ready day and night to help out the Wijnakkers. When he was in the neighborhood, he would visit them and always ask if they needed anything and then help get it.

Van Doorn worked out a special arrangement with the local farmers. As the official agricultural inspector for the region, it was his job to determine the tax on how much the farmers were bringing to market. So he counted less. In return for the smaller tax, the farmers would spare some extra crops, which van Doorn made available for Frans to pick up at the mill and occasionally at the local bakery. For instance, the farmers gladly gave one or two sacks of wheat or rye if van Doorn counted ten bags in place of twenty. Farmers of whom van Doorn knew to have a person hidden at their home could count on an extra discount. Then the weight of the pig to be slaughtered became much less too.

The farmers used to joke with van Doorn, saying, "You are a good Catholic with nine children. If you are short of something, it is your own fault."

Van Doorn's willingness to help, along with his official government position, made him a key asset for Frans.

As soon as German authorities or soldiers or other dangers were seen in Ravenstein, van Doorn would know and would warn Frans. Van Doorn's office was also where the mail and telegrams arrived. Since farmers and laborers like Frans seldom received letters or telegrams, communications coming to Frans from the Underground or going to people in hiding from relatives and friends in Amsterdam or other parts of the country would cause much alarm to the local officials looking to stay in line with the Nazi rule. So van Doorn became the keeper and distributor of any sensitive communications so as to divert attention away from Frans and what he was really doing.

Without the support of his wife Mien and the courageous help of Cor van Doorn, Frans would not have been able to do what he did. As 1943 moved forward and the war raged on, Frans's real business, placing and hiding Jews, was off and running.

Chapter Eight:
Adults Move in Too

Through acquaintances of one of the quartered soldiers from before the war, a Jewish couple contacted Frans in the early summer months of 1943. The couple, a banker and his wife, was still residing in Amsterdam. They sensed that times ahead would become very difficult, as the Nazis had increased the deportation of Jews to the concentration camps. They were scared and were looking to go into hiding, thus the communication to Frans. Since they were part of the Jewish Council, they still could travel around the country. As the Nazis had taken control of the major cities, Jewish residents were rounded up and herded into ghettos. The Jewish Council was the organization of Jewish leaders the Nazis formed to administer life in the ghettos.

The wife had asked to come for a visit to meet Frans and Mien in person and check out the living arrangements for life in hiding, She came out to Dieden the following week.

Frans told Mien that a woman would be coming on Sunday.

"What is she coming to do?" Mien asked.

"To buy eggs, I think," Frans replied.

"She's allowed to travel?"

"Yes, as far as I know," Frans responded.

The woman from Amsterdam came on Sunday. She conversed pleasantly with Frans and Mien about the current state of affairs and how life was in Amsterdam. The three ate in a room next to the Maas Dike embankment. The Jewish children ate in another room. Mien had asked the children to stay there and keep her own children with them.

After the meal, the woman said to Mien, "Madam, could I rent a room from you? You will get a lot of money for it. One room is enough for us. Then we will send some furniture here. I don't know if it is necessary. My husband is always saying that we can stay where we are. He was a German officer in the last war. But I don't trust the situation, so we want to be stored here." Hiding was often referred to as being stored.

"It will be difficult to give you a private room, but we are willing," Mien answered.

"What would it cost per year or per month?"

"We don't know just yet," Mien replied.

The woman continued. "Some people think the war will end this year, but I don't think that. Likely it will be 1944 or '45. But Hitler will lose. How about I pay twenty thousand guilders for '43 and '44, and then we will see further? The money is in a bank in Switzerland. Is there a notary here?"

"Yes, in Ravenstein," Frans answered.

"Then we can have the notary draw up the papers to complete this legally," the woman announced.

At that moment, the Wijnakker's daughter Nellie, a little girl of near four years old, came into the room. "This is our daughter, our oldest," Mien told the woman. Then Thijs, one of their sons, entered the front room.

Mien then said to both children, "You have to stay in the other room." Then Freetje and Fritsje came to get the children.

When the woman heard the two older children speak a little bit to Nellie and Thijs, she spoke up and said, "Those are Jewish children, aren't they?"

Frans and Mien nodded their heads to say yes.

"I can detect these children are German by their accent. You don't know what you have in your house. It is extremely dangerous."

"What do you mean?" asked Mien.

"My husband and I are intelligent adults," the woman continued. "We won't look through windows and would never stand in front of one either. You can tell children something like this, and in five minutes they forget. They'll start playing and will get in front of a window without even knowing it. People, you are playing a deadly game."

Frans and Mien said nothing as they took this all in.

"You have to listen" the woman pleaded. "You probably got these children from someone in Amsterdam. They have to leave before we come here. Otherwise, we won't come."

She kept insisting. Mien went to get tea, and at the door of the kitchen she turned around and firmly said, "Madam, listen. You can come when you want to, but the children stay. They have already been here awhile. We will not send them away."

The woman responded, "But, madam, the children are not too much for me. It is just much too dangerous for us and also for you. The people where the children came from will know of some other way to help them. Children are much easier to place than us adults."

"Send the children away? I won't do it. I cannot do that," Mien responded firmly.

The woman then said, "Madam, I can't do anything about that. But I think then it's best we do not come here."

They didn't. They were later transported away by the Nazis. On the way, the couple sent a postcard to the Wijnakkers. To send a card was very dangerous, as it could bring unwanted attention. Fortunately nothing came of it. The note in the postcard said: "The time has come. We left something for you with our neighbors." The neighbors in Amsterdam said later after the war, when asked, that they knew nothing about it.

✳

The fall of 1943 saw the business of giving refuge to Jews by Frans and Mien pick up, from taking people in to their own house to the building of a network with others in the local communities. The first adults they helped through this were a young married couple similar in age to them, Louis and Engelien (Lien for short) Baars. Lou was a quiet man of dignity and intelligence, and an architect by trade. Lien was a sociable woman with great devotion to her husband. Despite the stresses of the time that put her in a state of worry which never left her, she maintained a strong sense of perseverance. She worked as a secretary for the Jewish Council, the organization of Jewish leaders in the ghetto the Nazis set up and manipulated in their systematic efforts to deport all the Jews away. Being part of the Council bought her a little extra time. In the end, all this meant was the members of the Jewish Council would the last ones the SS would ship away.

The Baars couple had succeeded in escaping this last roundup of Jews from the ghettos of Amsterdam in late September 1943. They found a temporary shelter in the center of Amsterdam, knowing that they could not survive long staying in the city. Cok Ouweleen, likely part of the L.O., who along with her friend Mies Hoefsmit helped Freetje and Agnes escape from the city to the Wijnakkers, would be the source to help Lou and Lien.

She would accompany both by train, Lien first in October 1943 and Lou a short time later, out of Amsterdam to the province of North Brabant. And who would be her point of contact to help make arrangements for Lien and her husband, none other than Frans Wijnakker. Lou Baars became the first adult who took refuge in the Wijnakker house. He had no qualms about children being there. His uncle Jacobus Baars, also an architect, had taken in Shula's (Freetje) younger sister Hannah before the German occupation had begun. Once forced to be housed in the ghetto in Amsterdam, Lou could no longer work as an architect. Teaching children in the school set up in the ghetto is what he did and enjoyed.

But since he did not work for the Council, he had gone into hiding in Amsterdam within the ghetto first. He had already survived a few raids by the SS by hiding in closets and attics.

When Lou Baars came to the Wijnakker family in the fall of 1943, there was still no good hiding place in the house. Being an architect, Lou designed and worked with Frans to build a hiding room.

In a bedroom in the front of the house, a wall was built parallel to the wall of the adjoining living room. It was built between the steps to the upper level of the house and the outside wall of the house. This created what looked like a hallway between the bedroom and the living room. The hiding place was born. It had two entrances. In the real bedroom was a closet kept full of clothes, which had an invisible hatch that gave entrance to the hiding place. In the living room, there was also a hatch on the side of the fireplace wall that was almost invisible. Something could be placed in front of it. The hatch was made of cement so that if someone knocked on it during a house search, it would not be immediately clear that a hatch was there. At night is when Frans went about his crafty ways to secure the building materials needed. He and Lou made a good pair, working away to construct the hiding room that when done was the size of a small bedroom. Thank goodness the home was in the countryside where homes were not crowded next to each other, making such activity much less noticeable than in a city.

The Jews kept in the Wijnakker home only went into the hiding place when needed, such as when the doorbell unexpectedly rang, especially in the evenings, and, of course, if there was fear of a house search by the authorities. No one slept in the hiding place except Freetje and Fritsje, as they could not be awakened at night because they were such deep sleepers.

Frans and Mien Wijnakker also had four of their own small children. The children slept together in one small room. The plan that Frans and Mien decided was in the case of an emergency, such as a potential house search, the Jewish refugees would go into the hiding place and the four children would be laid in the beds of those people. This would serve as explanation as to why the beds were warm. At a later time, the radio was also placed in the hiding place.

When Lou Baars came to Dieden, he and Engelien had only been married a little over a year. The thinking was it would be best not to have them hidden together at the Wijnakker home, for a young couple together could lead to babies happening, which could create greater safety problems.

Word came first from the L.O. to Frans to work to find a placement for a young married woman. So he went to work with his new responsibility as a recruiter and broker to find this woman a reliable and safe place to hide—this woman being Lien Baars. A big assist in this first endeavor came from his ally Cor van Doorn, who would make a helpful connection for Frans. Cor would also help escort Lou Baars off the train in Ravenstein to the Wijnakker home a couple of weeks later.

In the town of Neerloon lived Cor's sister, Marie Louise. She had been a widow for only about two months. She had a small farm with four cows and had to live frugally. No widow's pension existed at that time. She had two children as well.

The support of the local priest, Father Simons, did not go further than his message: "It is God's will. God's will it is."

Frans went to visit Marie Louise. He said to her, "Marie, I may be able to support you a bit."

"Frans, you coming here to visit me is already a comfort. It's tough not having my husband around any more, but I know I have to go on. Luckily I still have my little farm. But I'm running the whole day trying to keep up with all the work for the farm and the house and not doing too well at it. I can't afford a farmhand to help either."

"Then I can be of help," he announced. "If you take a lady in to live in your house, I'll give you thirty guilders per week. She will do the housework, and then you can take care of the farm. I know this may sound generous and more than a normal salary, but this is important. Marie, she is a Jewish woman. She is only twenty-two years old, just married."

Frans continued his sales pitch. "If you agree, you cannot tell anyone. No one can know. And if you do it and you come to Peter at heaven's gate, he will say, 'Marie, come in quickly because you have done something wonderful. You saved someone's life.' But be careful, and don't talk about this to anyone because it is dangerous."

Marie agreed without hesitation.

The next evening, Engelien Baars arrived in Ravenstein by train. From there, she walked in the dark with Frans to Neerloon. About one month later, Frans went to visit to see how everything was going.

Marie Louise said to Frans, "We agreed that I would receive thirty guilders, but I thought you could do half of that. Thirty guilders is too much. The young lady keeps everything clean. She polishes the whole house."

"Marie, it will stay thirty guilders. You are really earning it. The risks are impossible to pay for."

"I know, but thirty guilders?"

"Marie, we will not talk about it further. It stays thirty guilders," Frans said firmly and with a smile.

"Now something else," she said. "When my husband was still alive, the priest came every Tuesday to drink and smoke a cigar. My husband has been dead for three months, and he has not visited. Do you know why?"

"No. Does he know you well and that you can't leave here?" Frans asked.

"Yes, he knows me. He has spoken with me. Could he be afraid to come? Or does he know I have a woman living in my house?" Marie wondered out loud.

"I don't think he knows that, and he doesn't have to know anything about that," Frans answered.

✳

Some days later, Father Simons came to see Marie Louise. It was difficult for him when he spoke to Marie at the door.

The priest said, "I feel so bad, Marie. It is almost impossible for me. A woman with two small children and still so young and alone. It is terrible. That is why I stayed away so long."

Marie told him, "I am financially well off, Father. You can know that. No need to worry."

Thinking of the priest as a holy and trustworthy person who could be told everything, she continued, "Father, I have a Jewish woman in the house who helps me."

"A Jewish woman?" he said with an astonished look on his face.

"Yes. I get thirty guilders per week for keeping her here, and she keeps my house clean. In the morning, I can go immediately to take care of the cows and also in the evening. The time flies by. I am not alone any more. I feel very lucky. Don't tell anyone."

"Yes, I had heard about it. How did you get her?" Father Simons asked.

"From Frans Wijnakker."

"Oh, I have heard about him before!" the priest exclaimed. "But a Jewish woman in the house. Do you know what the Germans will do if they find her? They will burn your house down. And I, I am the shepherd of the parish. So they will hang me from a tree, and then you will all be forced to stand there and watch. That is how it is, Marie. That Jewish woman, you have to get rid of her. Let that Wijnakker fellow see what he can do about her. But in Neerloon, there will not be any Jews living here. I don't want to stand for that! As I just explained, if the Germans find out, everything will be destroyed."

For Marie, like many people in the community, what the priest told you to do, you did. But in this case, Marie felt unhappy. She had expected Father Simons to say that she had done well.

Standing by the front door, Marie said, "Father, I can't do it. I can't send that woman away. I can't send her back to Wijnakker. I also don't know where he lives. She really doesn't know either."

When Father Simons got home, he phoned, as Frans would learn later, Marie's doctor who served the local area, Dr. Sluiters.

He said to the doctor, "Marie Louise, as you know, is a widow. What you may not know is that she has a Jewish woman in her house. She gets thirty guilders per week for that, which she can really use. But as you well know, if the Germans find out, if they search, they will burn the house down. And you know, Doctor, I am a fragile person. I am a heart patient, and I won't be able to sleep tonight from worry. Please go there and talk to Marie, and tell her that what she is doing is not right, that she has two children she needs to keep safe."

Dr. Sluiters then went to see Marie and said, "Marie, I heard from the Father about what you are doing. It is really not right. It is not sensible, and you also have two children you need to look after. The Germans will kill everyone if they find out. Send this woman out this evening on the dike. Then she can walk on it to the half broken-down church. Next to the church is the house where Wijnakker lives."

Marie submitted to the authority figures. With much regret, she asked Engelien Baars to go to Frans Wijnakker. "Continue going on the dike until you reach the Wijnakker's house," she told her. After that, she said a regretful farewell, and a scared and uncertain Engelien went out into the night to find her way.

That evening about midnight the doorbell rang at the Wijnakker house. Frans and Mien were still up. The people in hiding were all asleep. All the Jews in hiding had to leave their beds and go into the hiding room. Because the ringing of the bell was not accompanied by loud knocking on the door or some loud noise, Frans knew quickly that it was not the Germans. While he was unlocking the door, he heard a woman outside crying. He opened the door. It was Lien Baars, who recognized him immediately.

"I am luckily at the right address," she said between her tears as Frans appeared.

"Come in quickly," Frans said, for no light could show to the outside.

Mien was also at the front door, still in shock. She did not know Lien Baars. Engelien did not know that her husband was also hidden at the Wijnakker house. Frans had told her that he was somewhere in Limburg, a province south of Brabant. As mentioned before, young husbands and wives were, in most instances, placed in different locations to keep contact from occurring due to all the risks involved. Close placement was seen as too tempting.

Frans told the people in hiding, among whom some panic had broken out, that they could come out of the hiding place. To Lou Baars, he said, "Wait here. Someone who you know well has arrived."

Lou Baars did not wait and followed Frans to the front room. There he saw his wife, whom he had not seen for some time. Their reunion was, understandably, very emotional. Mien had, in the meantime, prepared coffee and heated chocolate milk to entertain everyone in the middle of the night. After the refreshments, everyone went off to bed.

Chapter Nine:
The House Fills Up

The reuniting of Engelien Baars with her husband in the wee hours of the morning was an emotional moment. As everyone headed back to bed, Mien said to Lou, "Bring the cot upstairs; then your wife can sleep in this room beside you."

"No, she can sleep with me," he said.

"That won't work in a single bed, will it?"

"Yes. When we were hidden in another place, we also had to do that. It works fine for one night," Lou explained.

In their own room, Frans and Mien discussed whether Lou and Lien Baars should stay together. The next morning, Lien Baars said, "I would really like to stay with my husband."

"Yes, we understand," said Frans, "but that really shouldn't happen. We will ask the man who makes decisions in these matters."

That was Long John from the Dutch Underground. His real name was never mentioned, just his code name of

Long John. A short time afterward, Frans met with Long John and got his approval for the young married couple to stay together since they did not have any children. Thus, Lou and Engelien Baars stayed at the Wijnakker home through the end of the war, but having a child would be another matter for later.

Later on, Sophia Roselaar, Engelien's mother and a widow, would also come to reside in the Wijnakker home. Her husband had died of a heart attack during the early raids in Amsterdam by the Nazis. She had been hidden with a family in the north of the country until that place was betrayed. *Betrayed* was the term the Dutch people used when word got out about someone being hidden in a certain place. This exposure usually meant danger and the threat of being captured by the German authorities, for both those hidden and those providing the hiding. Jos, Frans's brother, helped bring her out for safekeeping to his brother's home. Lou Baars tended to be the one to look after her. So Frans thought she was his mother.

In fact, throughout the fall and winter of 1943 and into 1944, the Wijnakker household took on more Jews in hiding. Sometimes the people there only stayed a night or two until Frans could place them in someone else's house in the local area. But some would come to stay, and before long the Wijnakkers usually had at least eight and up to ten regular residents beyond their own family of four children.

While conditions in the house were tight and simple, and sometimes a bit cold, there was always enough food, so no one went hungry. With the money Frans got from the Underground for helping to hide people, along with payments made by the adults in hiding who could afford it, Frans and Mien were able to provide clothing, food, and other necessary provisions for their refugee guests. Their big house was certainly running at full capacity.

Bertie Kroon was another person who came to hide and stay awhile in the Wijnakker house. She had an identification card in that name. Her actual name was Cacilie Levitus. She had come from Czechoslovakia via Germany to the Netherlands and had taken on a Dutch name in the process. When she came to the Wijnakker home, she was a girl of seventeen. She was a friend of Suzie Klazer, Agnes, having cared for Jewish children at the same nursery with her in Amsterdam.

Then there was Mr. Shapiro, who came to hide at the Wijnakker home. He was a pleasant man in his mid to late fifties who had come from The Hague. Once in a while, he would complain when the children were teasing him. Of course, they knew that so sometimes would tease him more just to have fun.

Mr. Shapiro enjoyed playing the violin and wanted to keep practicing if he could. From his request, Frans, on one of his occasional trips to The Hague, brought back a mute violin. It is an instrument whose sound is softened and only heard if you are very close to it. Mr. Shapiro was delighted and continued to play his violin in the attic.

Another person Frans and Mien took into hiding in their home was Mr. Bamberg. He had been hidden for a while in the town of Zaltbommel, a town in the province of Brabant some twenty-five miles or so west of Dieden. He had been hiding out there in a haystack, not exactly a safe place over the long haul. He snuck out and arrived in the tank of a milk truck. Prior to the war, he worked as a peddler, selling clothing and other goods from a pushcart. While he had no money, Frans and Mien took him in and built a little room in the attic for him.

He was a quiet man similar in age to Mr. Shapiro. With the exception of eating and visiting at times downstairs in the evening for some company, Mr. Bamberg stayed in his room in the attic. He knew he could not go outside and venture around. He liked to chew tobacco, which Frans supplied for him periodically. A coal bucket was set up in the kitchen for Mr. Bamberg to spit out his chewed tobacco. Unfortunately, he was not always a good aim, which sometimes upset the women in the house. He stayed until the end of the war. After the liberation, he returned to Amsterdam.

The Wijnakkers also took in Gustaaf and Eva Hess, a husband and wife without children. This couple came from the nearby town of Oss. They had first been in hiding in Batenburg, a village diagonally across from Dieden on the other side of the Maas River. They had suddenly not felt safe there anymore, as somebody was attempting to blackmail them. A letter had come to them, threatening to expose them to the authorities unless they started making payments. So they snuck away, crossed the river, and stayed with the Wijnakkers until the end of the war.

Mr. Hess was an economist. He was a quiet man of few words, a thinker. Mrs. Hess was the sociable person. She was very pleasant, and she kept up others' spirits.

Her efforts created a positive mood in the household—so important under such stressful circumstances.

The children and adults who had come to hide and reside in the Wijnakker home usually stayed inside much of the time and did not go out beyond the area of the house. They sometimes did exercises, such as calisthenics in the morning and read what they could, with the Bible the book most available. They helped around the house to keep it clean and looked after the Wijnakker children, with Freetje most of all helping care for the children. They also listened to the radio that was kept in the hiding room and would hear news about the war effort against the Germans, which created encouragement as 1944 progressed. During 1944, the Germans were on the retreat as Allied forces were making their advances in Europe. The D-Day invasion occurred in early June of 1944, which really began to loosen the Nazi grip over western Europe, giving hope to the people in occupied Netherlands and especially those forced into hiding.

Little problems sometimes came up in the household, from waiting to get into the bathroom to just getting on each other's nerves. This was not surprising with this many people living in the house and, for safety reasons, the chance to go outside greatly restricted on top of that. Frans usually worked hard to smooth things over and keep everyone's spirits up.

✳

With the two older girls of seventeen, Agnes and Bertie, efforts were made to allow them to work for other people. But such efforts sometimes ran into trouble.

For instance, while Agnes lived at the Wijnakkers, she stayed a lot with the Van Udens in Demen, the small town right next to Dieden. The Van Udens were a brother and sister in their seventies who lived together. Agnes served as a nurse's aid for them, caring for them and working to keep them and their house clean. These two siblings were country folk who were not used to bathing or changing their clothes often. While these habits created a challenge early on, Agnes was able to work through it and take good care of them. In fact, she found her stay there was more relaxing, as no one else was hidden in this place and, because of that, there was little fear of house searches.

One day as Agnes was on her way back to the Wijnakker house, someone who spoke German bicycled after her and came up alongside her.

He asked in German, "Do you live here?"

A shocked Agnes answered back in German, "No, I live in another village." They chatted for another minute, and Agnes then continued to ride ahead on her bicycle. The young man let her be.

The Zwanenbergs, a Jewish couple placed in hiding by Frans in the home of Piet Adriaans, saw the occurrence through a window and were upset with Agnes because she spoke with a German man. Agnes could not have done anything else because running away suddenly would have caused much more suspicion.

Frans heard about the incident from both the Zwanenbergs and Agnes. The decision was made to not have Agnes return just yet to work at the Van Udens' place. Frans was very worried about this potential betrayer in their midst, so he went to get more information about who this man was. He found out the man was a German soldier who had deserted from the army and was in hiding himself with a farmer in Ravenstein. When the shock passed, Agnes went back to work at the Van Uden house.

A short time later, Agnes would encounter another challenge. A neighbor who lived next to the Van Udens was working on his roof one day due to a storm that had blown tiles off the roof. He had seen Agnes next door before and saw her there this day. He asked Agnes if she would help him by handing him roof tiles that he would put back into place.

This neighbor, who was a bachelor, found Agnes quite attractive. After the work was finished, he boldly said to Agnes, "I would like to go out with you. How about this Sunday? We could get together and go for a walk?"

"Well, okay," Agnes replied hesitantly.

Agnes did not go outside that following Sunday. When she did not meet the neighbor, who knew where Agnes lived, he went biking to the Wijnakker house in Dieden. She remained hidden in the house, and he chose not to knock to see if she was there.

A few weeks later, the bachelor neighbor saw Agnes again outside at the Van Uden place. He saw dark hair starting to show through her white hair—her natural hair was starting to grow through the bleached hair. Laughing, he said, "You are becoming a dark girl. Soon you will look like a Jew."

The neighbor didn't know anything. He only knew that Agnes was recovering her health in Dieden, the message that had been spread around when Agnes first arrived in the area. Agnes was shocked at first by his comment but thought that the neighbor would probably forget his remark. So she just smiled, said nothing in return, and went back into the house. She would keep her distance from this man.

At a later time during a hot summer evening, Agnes was encouraged by her fellow children in hiding to go for a swim in the Maas River. Going at the dark of night was when they felt it would be safe to swim. Agnes, in her attempt to join them, nearly drowned for one simple reason: she really didn't know how to swim. The time in hiding was not a smooth process for Agnes, to say the least.

✳

After some time of living at the Wijnakker house that was overflowing, Bertie, the other seventeen-year-old young lady, went to live and work for the Arts family in Haren. Wim Arts had a small construction business and needed help in the household.

Frans told Wim, "Be careful. The situation is dangerous because she is Jewish. But you don't have to worry too much because she has a valid identification card, so you can let her go to the bakery. She could also go to church with you so people will assume she is Catholic. That is if you want to do so."

People in the neighborhood wondered how the family had gotten such a beautiful and hard-working girl. Some wondered if she was Jewish.

Bertie always told the same story: "My mother is alive, but my father died. Things are difficult in Amsterdam, and now I've ended up in Haren." She never talked about Dieden or the Wijnakkers. She always said she had come to be in Haren through acquaintances in Tilburg.

One day as Bertie was riding her bicycle in Haren, a local policeman came up on his bicycle and pulled next to her. "I haven't seen you before," he said. "You look like such a beautiful city girl. I would like to go out with you one evening."

Bertie kept on her way, yet the policeman continued to ride beside her. She stopped next to the Arts' house. "We could make a date sometime?" the policeman asked.

"I'll have to think about it," Bertie said softly. The policeman then rode away, mentioning he'd come back soon to find out. She immediately told Mr. Arts about the incident, but he had actually seen it from his house. That evening he went to see Frans.

Wim Arts sounded stressed as he explained what had happened with Bertie and then said to Frans, "Pick her up from my house quickly. She's been betrayed."

"I don't believe that," Frans replied. "No one has been betrayed. She is a pretty girl. This policeman is a skirt chaser and thought that maybe he could get her to go out with him." Frans could not be convinced at first the matter was more than that. He knew of this policeman and knew that he was married. After Wim persisted, Frans agreed to take action.

A telegram was arranged. The story was it came from Amsterdam telling Bertie that her mother was sick and she needed to come home immediately. So Bertie visited everyone in her Haren neighborhood to say good-bye. Once or twice as a tear was shed, she would say to people, "I have to say good-bye. Mother is seriously ill, and I don't know if I'll be able to come back here any time soon."

As part of the plan, Bertie then went to the train station in Oss and took the train in the direction of Den Bosch. Frans, who was coming back from Amsterdam, met her there. Together they traveled to Dieden. Frans even had Bertie write a short letter to the Arts saying that her mother was very sick and she needed coupons for butter and sugar. Bertie gave her address in Amsterdam. From Haren came coupons and also butter that Cor van Doorn intercepted and shared with Frans. The suspicions that Bertie was Jewish disappeared.

A short time later, Frans arranged a new place for Bertie. She stayed until the end of the war in Ravenstein with the Van Aar family, who had a small grocery store. Sometimes at night she would come by the Wijnakkers to visit. The overall situation was not easy for Bertie, but she was a strong person, and she persevered.

BACK ROW: SHULA (FREETJE) WITH HER BROTHER
AVRAHAM (FRITSJE) HOLDING BABY INEKE JUST AFTER
LIBERATION BY ALLIED FORCES IN SEPTEMBER 1944.
IN THE FRONT ROW ARE THE FOUR
WIJNAKKER CHILDREN, LEFT TO RIGHT:
FRANS, JR., NELLIE, THIJS, AND JAN.

FRANS AND MIEN WIJNAKKER IN 1945. THE JOB WAS
DONE AND LIFE WAS STARTING TO RETURN TO NORMAL.

The Baars family pays a visit to the home of the Wijnakkers, late 1940's.

Left to right: Engelien Baars holding son Bernard with daughter Leah (Ineke) standing in front of Frans and Mien.

Frans Wijnakker in 1993, one year before his death.

The plaque honoring Frans and Mien Wijnakker in the Avenue of the Righteous at Yad Vashem in Jerusalem, Israel.

FRANS IN FRONT OF THE CITY HALL IN RAVENSTEIN,
NETHERLANDS IN THE SUMMER OF 1984, GETTING
READY TO GO IN THE LOCAL PARADE FOR BEING
OFFICIALLY HONORED BY YAD VASHEM AS ONE
OF THE RIGHTEOUS AMONG THE NATIONS.

LEAH "INEKE" BAARS REUNION WITH THE FIVE
WIJNAKKER CHILDREN, MAY 27, 2009.

LEFT TO RIGHT: THIJS, JAN, IRENE, LEAH
BAARS, FRANS, JR., AND NELLIE.

LEAH "INEKE" BAARS RE-MEETS SHULA SCHWARZ
(FREETJE) IN HAIFA, ISRAEL IN APRIL 2010; SOME
65 YEARS SINCE THEY WERE LAST TOGETHER.

FRANS AND MIEN WIJNAKKER HOLDING
BABY INEKE, LATE 1944.

MARTY AT THE END OF A STORYTELLING PRESENTATION WHERE HE REVEALS HIS MEANINGFUL PERSONAL CONNECTION, BABY INEKE, HIS WONDERFUL WIFE LEAH BAARS.

THE WIJNAKKER HOME AS IT WAS IN THE 1940'S.

MIEN AND FRANS WITH THEIR FIVE CHILDREN,
POSTWAR IN 1948. L. TO R.: THIJS, NELLIE, MIEN
(SEATED), IRENE, FRANS (SEATED), JAN, AND FRANS, JR.

FRANS WIJNAKKER, JR. AND HIS WIFE IRENE IN
FRONT OF THE REMODELED HOUSE OF TODAY
THEY NOW OWN—THE HOME WHERE THEIR
PARENTS' RESCUE EFFORTS OCCURRED.

Chapter Ten:
The Brokering
Business Expands

Luckily Frans had Mien's help in maintaining a very full household of Jewish residents. In the meantime, he actively searched for new hiding places as more Jews were coming in need of refuge.

Once, Frans visited an old woman who lived a stone's throw from where he lived. Her name was Janske van den Berg. Her husband, Grad, had died some time before. She had two grown daughters living with her. Janske did not have any money, as was true of a lot of people at that time.

One day Frans went to see Janske. As he came to her house, he saw she had a rooster tied to a piece of string. "Yes, he is tied up," Jankse started to explain. "Otherwise, he constantly chases the chickens. I'll slaughter him for Christmas. He's a good one. If I were to sell him today, I believe I could get fifteen guilders for him."

Frans jumped in. "I want to give you twenty-five guilders for him."

"Yes?" Janske responded in disbelief as she picked up some corn with her bent, arthritic fingers. "Here he is." She grabbed the rooster and gave him to Frans.

"I'll bring you the twenty-five guilders this evening," Frans said as he left with the rooster.

"That's good," replied a smiling Janske.

That evening Frans returned to see Janske. He took a good look around her house to see how it was laid out. Janske sat by the fire, warming her hands. She picked up a piece of wood and threw it on the fire. On top of that she threw a handful of coal. Smoke hung inside the house.

"Janske, how is it going financially with you? Do you have enough?"

"Oh, yeah, we're doing okay," she answered. "It's not as good as when Grad was alive, but no one comes to ask me if I can make it. Luckily, I have a little land. We can live from what the land brings forth."

"Yes, but, Janske, you don't have to," Frans stated.

"That's nice for you to say so, but you still go once in a while to trade in Amsterdam. Naturally I can't do that with my old legs," she said.

"Janske, I know a solution," Frans announced. "You will get eighty guilders per week from me, and you won't have to do much for that."

"But for that amount, I should be doing something," she said. "I would like to do a lot for eighty guilders!"

"Oh, here is the twenty-five guilders for the rooster," Frans said.

In near disbelief, Janske replied, "I haven't seen twenty-five guilders together in one place for a long time, probably years ago."

"You don't believe it, and yet it is so. Eighty guilders per week and you don't have to do too much for it," he said again.

"What's involved then?" she asked.

"Take two people into your home about your age, sixty years old. It is a man and a woman."

"But how is that possible? Eighty guilders for that?"

"They are rich, and they want to live here," he replied.

"Rich people? They would not want to live here," she said with much doubt in her voice.

Frans spoke softly. "Janske, they are Jews. The husband is an artist. They are Jewish people."

"But Hitler won't be coming here," Janske said, laughing. She did not know then how dangerous the situation was.

"Frans, you are looking at my house as if it is very large, but half of it is the barn for the cows and pigs. The front of the house is not so big. Come and look."

She started to guide Frans around the house. "You don't have to look to the left because my daughters sleep there. That is the room above the cellar." She then pushed a door open. "This is the living room." In it were a table and a couple of very old chairs that looked like one could no longer sit on them.

"This is my bedroom, and you cannot sleep upstairs because you'd fall through the ceiling. I can't put the people in the hay in the barn."

"No, that wouldn't work. But, Janske," Frans said, "if you were to put your bed in front of the window, then the bed for those people would fit into the back of the room."

"But how can that be with me already in the bedroom?" Janske exclaimed.

"Why not?"

"They won't want that," she answered.

"Yes, they will want it," he said. "They will be happy that they can come here."

"But you can't move my bed. It is nailed into the floor."

Frans suggested another idea. "You know what? We still have a single bed. That bed will go in front of the window. Your bed will then be taken out, and the other bed for these people can then fit into the back of your bedroom."

"In my bedroom? I don't care, but what about these people? And when will they come?" she asked.

"They are already here at my house. They can come soon. First, I'll come tomorrow evening and bring the bed in the dark."

"Now, go ahead. I hope it goes well. I'll pray for that tonight, that it all goes well."

"Yes, you do that. Thank you," Frans said as he departed.

The following evening Frans brought the bed and arranged things in the bedroom. He had told the artist and his wife that they'd be staying with good people, but they were poor. They would eat what the land produced. They would be taken care of but not spoiled. "Now you will learn what real poverty is," was how Frans summed up the situation.

Later that evening, the man, wearing a derby hat, and his wife walked with Frans to Janske's house. They quickly felt at home. When Frans checked in two weeks later, they were feeling very satisfied.

"She is a sweet woman, and the daughters are also nice," the couple said. They ate well, with everything coming from the land.

Sometime later Janske needed to go to confession for Christmas and asked Frans, "I think the priest knows I have Jews in my house. If he asks if it is true, what should I say?"

"That depends on what he asks."

"And if he asks me how much I get for this, what do I tell him?"

"Say thirty guilders."

"Yes, but you can't lie in a confessional. That can't be."

"Janske, go ahead. It's no problem."

"But then I won't be able to celebrate Christmas, will I?" she said with concern.

"You'll have to do it. Otherwise, you really won't have a good Christmas. You see, you're really doing something special that the good LORD appreciates," Frans said convincingly.

She then went home, and when Frans asked later how confession went, she laughed and told him nothing had been asked about that. Yet the money she received continued to gnaw at her.

"You told me that when I arrive in heaven at Peter's gate, he would pull me inside. But he won't pull hard if he already knows something—that I got eighty guilders to take these people in my home, eighty guilders from people in distress," Janske said to Frans.

He explained, "Peter will be waiting for you and them at the gate. Jesus could show himself in the person of a drifter asking for help. You will all be in good hands."

❋

As part of his brokering work, Frans also called upon another local woman, Mien van Uden. She had a large family where a new baby was born every year. Help was needed in the household but too expensive to get.

"Mien, I can get a helper for you. She's a girl from Amsterdam. Conditions there are bad, and there is not enough to eat. You don't have to pay anything, and you'll receive ten guilders in addition while she is here," Frans told her.

"Frans, that sounds too good to be true," Mien van Uden said.

"It is true," Frans reassured her. "Now, she is a Jewish woman. Don't talk to anyone about that."

"And if people come here to get milk?" she asked.

"That doesn't matter," he said. "The girl knows her story. Things are going badly in Amsterdam."

Mien agreed, and shortly afterward Fien Vos arrived. This so-called young girl had been temporarily hidden in Dieden and had a daughter herself who was three years old. That daughter came to be hidden at the Wijnakker house, although not for long, as the Wijnakkers had a very full house. The little girl was then hidden with a family in Klein-Amerika in the province of Limburg.

All went well, and Fien Vos stayed until the war's end.

Next, together with Long John, Frans went to see Truuske de Koster in Demen. She lived in a large house next to the parsonage. Her father lived with her. He had dementia.

When she greeted the two gentlemen, Truuske turned to Frans and said, "I think you are at the wrong place. I can't buy anything. Father Simons doesn't know that everything is costing more. He also complains about other things on top of that."

"Yes, Truuske, that's the way he is," Frans said. "But we did not come to sell you anything. You will get sixty guilders per week, maybe as much as eighty, if you can help us. I think you have two empty rooms upstairs, right?"

"Yes. But eighty guilders?" she said in puzzlement.

"Listen well, Truuske," Frans said softly yet firmly, knowing that Truuske was a good Christian woman. "We want to bring a couple to stay with you in your house for a while. They are Jewish, and it is very dangerous right now. If you will do this, you will get to heaven, and they will say, 'Truuske, you did good in the world.'"

Long John joined in the conversation. They spoke further about the dangers involved in hiding Jews. Stories were appearing in the newspapers recently about what happened when Nazis found Jews in hiding. Usually those in hiding along with those who helped them hide would be arrested by the SS and shipped off to concentration camps in Poland.

Undeterred, Truuske invited Frans and Long John in to see her empty rooms. "Come up and look. I don't know if it is good enough."

They went upstairs to see. Walking around in the rooms, Frans said, "Truuske, this is good."

"They are naturally used to better things?" she asked.

"That is not a problem," Frans replied. "Look. From here they have a view of the village of Batenburg and the Maas River. They will not be able to go outside and should also not be allowed downstairs. Nobody can see them. They know that themselves. You'll bring the food upstairs and put a toilet pot here if you have one. Otherwise, we will take care of that."

Truuske agreed. She did not have to ask her father. Luckily, he knew from nothing. But then she raised an issue. "But the house does not belong to me. I will have to ask permission from the Father. We live here free of rent. Come back tomorrow; then I'll know more."

Frans had not thought of that. He knew if she went to the priest, her home as a shelter would never work out.

"Truuske," Frans said, "we will go to see Father Simons for you. If things are all right, we will return this evening. Visiting here during the day for two days in a row is too obvious."

Frans and Long John went directly to the priest. Tonia, his maid, as was usual, opened the door. She announced, "Father, Wijnakker and another man are here. Could they speak with you?"

"Let them come in," he answered.

"Oh no, Wijnakker. When I see you, it usually means trouble for me," Father Simons said, shaking his head in dismay. He then stopped so he wouldn't continue to lament away, which he found easy to do when he saw Frans Wijnakker.

Long John then introduced himself. "I am Jan Van Lanschot."

"Oh, are you a son of Willem? From the bank?" the priest asked.

"Yes," Long John answered.

"And your mother, is she still alive?"

"Yes, she is still alive," Long John replied.

Father Simons continued to ask questions about his family. Jan Van Lanschot, Long John's real name, answered them easily.

"And Marlies?"

"She married an attorney."

"That is very good," the priest said. "Boy, oh boy, those attorneys, they can make as much money as they want. Now when I see the Wijnakker sitting there, I think I know what this will be about."

"Then Frans can tell you better himself," said Long John, gesturing to Frans to go ahead and speak.

"Father, you are getting new neighbors," Frans stated matter-of-factly.

"Where?" the Father asked.

"Next door, with Truuske," Frans replied.

"With Truuske?" the priest said with surprise.

"Yes, Father," Frans confirmed.

"How is that possible? They only get six guilders per week. How can they support more people?" Father Simons asked.

"Not a problem. These neighbors will pay," Frans replied.

"Where do they come from? And is he an attorney?" the priest asked.

Frans named some far-off place and explained the man was a grain dealer.

The priest continued, "That also pays well. But did Truuske agree to take them?"

"Yes, she wants to do it out of neighborly love," Frans said.

"Yes, Wijnakker, that's what you always say," Father Simons responded. "It is not neighborly love. It is taking big risks. Wijnakker, you'll carry on only so long until the Germans find out something, and I'll be the first to go."

"They don't even know where you live," Frans replied.

"I hear you, but you still continue to place people," the priest lamented.

"Truuske sent us here. She can't ask for herself. But she wants your okay."

"It is terrible, terrible," Father Simons again lamented. But the priest could not reject it because he did not want to lose face in Van Lanschot's presence. The Van Lanschot family was a fairly well-known and well-to-do family in Holland. He then said, "Wijnakker, you won't listen anyway. Do what you want to do."

"It is all right then?" Frans asked.

"Do what you want to do," the Father responded with a sigh.

"Then they will come," Frans exclaimed. He and Long John then quickly left to tell Truuske.

✳

The grain dealer and his wife then went into hiding at Truuske's house in Demen. They had been hidden at a home in the town of Megen, the home of the brother and sister of Janske's deceased husband. But that arrangement was only temporary.

A short time later, Frans checked in to see how everything was working. The couple in hiding expressed satisfaction with their new arrangement. Truuske, however, expressed concern to Frans about how much she was being paid. She said, "Frans, forty guilders is enough. I want to help out of neighborly love. I earn too much now."

"Truuske, it was agreed," Frans responded. "They can pay it easily, and they want to pay it. They are satisfied with you. You are such a good cook. I hear they sometimes give you something extra. We won't talk about it anymore. It is not only about money. Money is not the measure of everything. Helping these people is a good deed."

✳

A tense day occurred for the grain dealer and his wife a short time later. News spread that the mayor of Oss was murdered in Ravenstein. Van Doorn sent warnings. Frans prepared for house searches. The grain dealer and his wife panicked and fled in the evening to the Wijnakker house and took refuge in their hiding place. To Frans, fleeing was not an intelligent move now that house searches were a real possibility in 1944. But fear has little intelligence.

The wife had a pill with her, and she said to Mien, "If there is knocking on the door and it is the Germans, I will take that pill. Then they won't have to take me with them because I'll already be dead."

Mien wanted to throw away the pill, but the woman refused to hand it over. She kept it with her in the hiding place. They stayed the night, and when the danger had lessened, they went back to Truuske's house again.

The grain dealer and his wife were fine. They ended up staying put until the end of the war. When the wife got sick, Truuske was ready to help day and night to nurse her back to good health.

✳

Another example of Frans's brokering work involved a Jewish child from Poland. The child came eventually to hide with a family in the very small town of 't Wild, just north of the small city of Oss—all in the same province of Brabant. Frans had first attempted to take the child for safekeeping with a priest in that area. The priest had a large garden surrounded by a tall wall. This child especially needed fresh air.

The priest's response to Frans was abrupt. "A Jew in a priest's house—that cannot be. Don't you understand that, Wijnakker!"

After that, Frans went to visit a convent in the area. He said to Mother Superior of the convent, "They will never find the child here. This place is surrounded by tall hedges and a moat. Germans won't come here."

"We would like to help you," said Mother Superior, "but I don't dare. I have the responsibility for all the sisters, and you don't know what might happen. The whole place, the convent, could be destroyed."

The Van Erp family lived close to the Wijnakkers. On occasion, if the place was full at the Wijnakker house, they helped out by taking a Jew into hiding for one or two nights. Mrs. Van Erp, Mieke, had told her sister Truus, who lived in 't Wild, about what was going on in her own house and at the Wijnakker house. She mentioned that she was scared at night and could not sleep when people in hiding were at her house. But she didn't want to refuse to help when a temporary arrangement was needed.

Learning about Truus from her sister Mieke, Frans went to visit Truus in 't Wild.

Truus explained to Frans, "I heard from Mieke about what you're doing, but that doesn't matter. I won't tell anyone. But that is really something at your house, with all those Jews."

"Yes, it is not easy, but there they are," Frans said. Then he asked, "Do you know of a home, a farmer for example, who has children and to whom I can bring a Jewish child to be kept?"

"That is asking a lot," Truus said. "I don't know a lot of farmers. But is this such a problem for you?"

"Yes, that child needs to go outside and be able to play in the sun. The person who takes the child in will get ten guilders per week," Frans explained.

Eventually Truus said, "Frans, if you are at the end of your rope and you haven't found a place in eight days, then bring the child here. I already have thirteen children. Where thirteen children can eat, fourteen can also eat."

Eight days later Frans brought the child to Truus and her family. The child stayed until the end of the war and became like one of the family. When it was time to say good-bye, it was hard to say farewell for all involved.

Throughout 1943 and well into 1944, these stories were examples of the brokering activity that became the main focus of Fran's life. It was his work—work filled with great risk. During this time period, especially in the big cities, Rauter and his SS forces were relentless in hunting down Jews they heard were in hiding. As mentioned in Chapter Four, the Nazis also paid bounties to people who reported suspicious activity that led to the capture of people in hiding, especially Jews, with the group of bounty hunters known as the Henneicke Column quite successful at tracking down Jews in hiding. Great way to make extra money during these hard economic times in the Netherlands.

In addition, Rauter and his SS came down hard using brutality, sometimes executions, in response to violent acts from the various Dutch resistance organizations. Despite the strong-armed tactics meant to intimidate the Dutch citizenry, the resolve of the resistance movement remained steadfast. So too did Frans's resolve for the hiding work he was doing, but he became much more aware of the dangers he faced from when he first started on this journey.

Chapter Eleven:
Baby Ineke

While Frans was quite busy looking for places to take in the Jewish refugees that came his way through the Underground, he still had to contend with and care for the people hiding in his own home. In particular, a major concern came up related to Lou and Engelien Baars.

One day in the fall of 1943, Mien said to Frans about the Baars couple, "I think they are having difficulties. This morning when I came into the room she was sitting in his lap. He looked worried, and she had been crying."

"We can't meddle, and it will probably pass. Remember, they're just a young couple," Frans replied.

Actually Engelien Baars was twenty-seven at this time, and her husband, Lou, was nearly five years older. Frans always thought they were a young couple in their early twenties, not realizing they were close in age to Mien and himself.

Then a couple of weeks later, in October 1943, after Frans returned from a trip to Amsterdam, Engelien approached him alone and in an anxious manner. Normally she would ask him questions about how things were in Amsterdam, such as if Frans had heard if a person was still there and what the situation was like in the city. This time she immediately started to cry and sat down next to Frans. She had a secret she could no longer keep secret.

"Such a young woman—why do you cry so much? What's the matter?" Frans asked.

"Oh, something awful. If I tell you, we'll have to leave here," Engelien responded through her tears.

"Leave? Says who?" an incredulous Frans responded. He thought he already knew anyway.

"I am pregnant," she finally blurted out. Engelien Baars was now at least five months pregnant. She was a woman small in stature, and she had not been showing much. Yet she knew she could not hide that fact much longer.

"Do you have to cry about that? You're married. It couldn't be avoided in that single bed," Frans said.

She started to laugh a little through her tears and continued to talk. "But I am five months along. I've kept it hidden, but now I had to tell. Do I have to leave?"

"Not according to me," Frans replied. "But I can't make that decision. Long John comes soon, so I will check it out with him. I think everything will be okay. No need to make any move right now."

Frans consulted with Long John. The discussion explored the possibility of moving Lien out of the area for the birth to be done somewhere else. Such arrangements would mean likely splitting up the family.

But Long John did not want to dictate a decision in this situation. He turned to Frans and said, "I think it is best that you and Mien decide want works best here." The decision was made to allow Lou and Engelien Baars to stay at the Wijnakker house.

There were bigger issues to be worked out regarding this childbirth situation, left in the hands of Mien and Frans to handle. They discussed it often, usually in the late evenings when they were in the privacy of their own bedroom. That was, in fact, the only private place they had.

The subject was regularly discussed with Lou and Lien Baars too. They were all in agreement that it would be best if Frans and Mien could claim the child as their own. Then the baby could be outside in a crib, be taken for medical checkups, and be seen as one of the family. Frans, Jr., had been born in 1942 and was sixteen months old at this time, and Mien was not expecting when Engelien announced her pregnancy. So the scenario discussed was possible to do.

While Mien was not expecting, one aspect worried her. Frans and Mien were both still young. They had had their babies quickly, as was normal at that time in a Catholic family. One after the other was born, five children within six years: Joke, Nellie, Thijs, Jan, and in 1942, Frans, Jr. Joke, the oldest daughter, died in 1939 at the age of three due to a lung infection. The pill did not exist in those times, while Catholic doctrine restricting birth control did. Since Mien was still in her reproductive years, as a devout Catholic, the belief was she and her husband were supposed to continue to try and have babies.

One evening Mien said to Frans, "Listen, I'm worried. I won't go to hell for the Jews. Abstinence is not allowed, as you know."

"Yes, but now it's okay," said Frans.

"Now, now it's not okay!" objected Mien.

Frans thought to himself, *I don't know what to do. I can't be separate, and I can't do without my wife's help, especially under these extraordinary circumstances.* But before Frans had finished thinking, Mien was able to cool herself down and offer a plan, one with which Frans was in total agreement.

The plan was she would ask her local doctor for a referral. She would claim to have such stomach pains that it would not be good health-wise to get pregnant right now. If she could get her doctor to give this medical referral, the church would likely allow for a period of abstinence until she regained her health.

Her local doctor, Dr. Sluiters, recommended she see a specialist in Nijmegen, the largest city in the local area. She did. At the visit, Mien told the doctor in Nijmegen, someone she heard was trustworthy, everything—that they had Jews hidden in their house, that one of the women in hiding was expecting a baby, that Mien and her husband would register the baby as their own child.

She then asked the doctor, "How can we make this work? We are still young. We only have four children, and we want some more later on but not now."

The doctor listened intently and then went to get a priest to come to his office. The Nijmegen priest asked

Mien, "Does the priest of your parish know you are hiding Jews in your home?

"Yes, he knows," she replied.

"I'll write you a letter, in Latin, explaining your situation as you described, and you'll have your priest sign it. Then there will not be any babies for you as long as the war lasts." Mien smiled and thanked the priest and the doctor for their help.

That evening Mien arrived home and reported to Frans the good news that happened in her meeting with the doctor and the priest who joined in. "If our priest also signs this note, we won't have to have babies as long as the war lasts."

"That's something!" Frans exclaimed.

"Yes, but you also have to show faith," Mien said firmly. "So please go to confession this Saturday evening and give Father Simons this note and ask him to sign it."

Saturday Mien reminded Frans to go to confession. He had actually not planned to go but went because of her urging.

In the confessional, upon seeing Frans, Father Simons blurted out, "Oh no! When I see you coming, I get afraid."

"Oh yeah?" Frans responded calmly.

"Is it about the Jews?" the priest inquired.

"Sort of," replied Frans.

"Not here. That can't be talked about here," the priest said anxiously.

"Where then?" Frans asked.

"Later come to the parsonage. Come this evening shortly after six," Father Simons instructed. "Oh no, if it is about that dangerous activity you're involved with, it is terrible!"

Then at the Holy Communion, the usual end of confession, Frans tried to pass the special note he had to the priest. But the Father said unrelentingly, "At the parsonage. Not here."

That evening just after six, Frans came to the parsonage. The maid, Tonia, opened the door and said, "Hello, Wijnakker."

"I would like to speak with the Father for a minute," Frans requested.

"That's not possible," Tonia answered. "The Father did confessions, and then he became tired. But if you want to have him do a Mass or something, I'll pass on the message. I can tell him that in the morning."

"But I really have to talk with him," Frans responded with concern.

"Is it urgent?" she asked.

"Yes, it is quite urgent," he stated firmly.

"Now then I'll go ask for you," obliged Tonia.

When Frans heard the priest tell Tonia to let him come in, Frans moved quickly into the study where Father Simons was sitting. The father saw him and said, "Come close, Wijnakker. I'm a little hard of hearing. Tell me what's on your mind this time."

"Father, I thought that we would be speaking privately?" Frans asked. Tonia was in the room arranging some flowers. She wanted to hear what was going on. The priest then asked her to leave.

After she stepped away, he turned to Frans and said, "Okay, tell me what's up."

"I have a Jewish woman who is pregnant," Frans blurted out.

"What! Expecting a baby!" the priest exclaimed.

He then lifted himself out of the chair with his arms raised to the ceiling and went into a rant. "There you have it. All those strange people in your house, and still it couldn't be any other way. Everything has to be done by Wijnakker! And look where it got you, you idiot! We'll all be blown up by the Germans. How could you do this to me! It is awful!"

Father Simons then fell back in his chair. He paused momentarily and then continued, "And your wife, what does she have to say about it? Or doesn't she care either?"

The reaction was so harsh that Frans was thinking the pastor probably believed that the child was out of wedlock or thought Frans was the father. He then jumped in and said to the priest, "Father, you're not understanding me. That child is from a Jewish married couple."

The priest's face cleared. "Then you want to have it baptized?"

Frans was always respectful of the faith or lack of faith of his people in hiding. He had no problem with that. There were more important problems to worry about. God would not have wanted it. "No, they don't want that," he replied.

"What then?" the priest asked.

"Father, listen, and I'll tell you quickly. If you don't interrupt me, you'll know it immediately."

He continued. "The baby will be born in February, and I want to record the birth at city hall falsely."

"Don't you trust them there?" Father Simons inquired.

"It's not about that, about city hall. I trust them, but they are not concerned in this. I want to falsely report the child," Frans repeated.

"Record it falsely?" the Father wondered out loud.

"Yes, I want to record this baby as my child. What happens then is that he or she would be our child. If the Germans come, then the child would be ours and might be saved," explained Frans.

The clergyman shook his head in disbelief and said, "If the Germans come, do you know what will happen then? We'll all be destroyed, and I would go first. The Germans, they are nasty. You've heard that!"

Frans persisted. "Yes, Father, but that is not what this is about. The idea is that the child will be saved if they come. My wife can then take the baby for a medical consultation, and the child can go outside in the sun."

The priest calmed down and seemed sunken in prayer. Suddenly he said, "Our dear LORD probably finds that okay. He thinks it is good." In a raised voice, he continued, "But it is forbidden to not follow the law. But, Wijnakker, who doesn't listen to me, he goes his own way anyway. He can go ahead with it. That's the way it is, isn't it?"

"But our dear LORD, he'll think it's all right?" Frans asked.

"Yes, I believe so," the Father answered. "He'll approve of it. Are you satisfied now?"

"Not yet," Frans said.

"What else?" the priest asked with a sigh.

Frans gave the priest the Latin note he had from Nijmegen and requested, "Father, would you sign this?"

As the Father went to open the envelope, he noticed the seal was broken. "You opened it already?" the priest said with another sigh.

"Yes, but I couldn't read it," Frans explained.

"No," said the priest while he grinned, "that you don't know. I am a scholar. I can read Latin." He then looked over the note.

"Where did you get this?" Father Simons asked in a suspicious tone.

"I didn't get it. My wife did," Frans replied. "She went to see a doctor in Nijmegen, but the note is from a priest there."

"From a priest?" responded the Father, looking puzzled.

"You need to sign it, and when the note is signed, my wife will return it to that priest. He said that in the next year we then would be okay to not have a baby," Frans explained.

"I'll tell you immediately. That couldn't be a priest. That's not a priest. Do you know what this is?" asked Father Simons, waving the letter at Frans.

"No," replied Frans.

"Then I won't say anyway. What this is, one cannot write that. That is not allowed if one is really a priest!" He then gave the note back to Frans and said, "I won't sign it."

Shortly after, Frans then met with a priest from the town of Megen, asking for an explanation about the note.

After glancing quickly at the note, the Megen priest smiled and said, "This letter describes the sexual practices you should follow to minimize the chances for pregnancy, advising you and your wife to follow the rhythm method. I don't have to read the whole letter to figure that out. If you use this method well and your wife is healthy, then the chances are good that you won't have babies while the war lasts—though no guarantees."

Afterward, Frans filled in Mien about his ordeal with Father Simons along with what he learned from the priest out of the Megen parish. Mien felt better about what she heard and was now ready to move forward to help the Baars couple have their child.

✳

In the winter months leading up to the birth of the baby, when Mien went out into public, she did so with a pillow tucked next to her stomach underneath her clothes so she appeared to be pregnant.

The next challenge to work out was how the child would be born. With the help of Cor van Doorn, arrangements were made for the baby to be born in the convent right outside Ravenstein. Lien Baars could stay for several nights. Having the birth at the Wijnakker home with so many children and adults hidden in the house was not a good idea.

Mother Superior of the Ravenstein convent wanted to talk with Frans ahead of time. She said to him, "You have to promise one thing with your hand over your heart:

that you will never tell anyone. This situation is so very dangerous."

"Don't worry," Frans reassured her. "No one knows, and no one will ever know."

Frans had to arrange transportation. He asked an acquaintance to drive Engelien Baars to the convent outside of Ravenstein, only giving a little information that the driver was to take a pregnant woman from his house to the convent.

Frans also had to work to find a doctor who would handle the delivery. He went first to see the local doctor who did rounds in Ravenstein and surrounding villages, Dr. Sluiters. This doctor knew that Frans had people hidden. One time he had pulled a tooth of a Jewish woman who was hiding in the area. So Frans asked the doctor for his assistance.

Dr. Sluiters responded, "Boy, oh boy, Frans, you are already so involved, and now this too. When the baby is born, they will ask who delivered it. Confess, they'll say to me."

"I don't know what will happen then," said Frans. "But she still needs to deliver the baby soon."

"I would like to do this, but I have to worry about my family. I don't dare risk their safety," the doctor explained as he declined getting involved.

Frans then sought out Dr. Baptist in Megen. Dr. Baptist was known in the area not only for his fine medical knowledge but also for his kind and helpful ways. He was greatly revered because of the quality care he provided. Often Dr. Baptist bicycled late in the evening, and even in the middle of the night to see patients. Even when his bike, which was his only means of transportation, was stolen, the good doctor said that there was someone who needed a bicycle even more than he did. He gave help, literally, for an apple or an egg.

Dr. Baptist could also make his own medicines so was often the source for medications in the area. This was a good way for him to make some money; otherwise, he would have been bankrupt. Yet he wound not charge patients for medications if they could not afford to pay. Not surprisingly, a statue was later placed in Megen honoring the doctor's untiring work for sick people.

By coincidence, Frans met the doctor's assistant on the road as he was coming upon Megen. Frans had heard that he was also trustworthy. Frans said, without indicating that he was hiding more than one person, "I have a Jewish woman in my house."

"Who are you?" the doctor's assistant asked.

"Frans Wijnakker."

"Oh, I've heard about you and what you are doing," the doctor's assistant said in a matter-of-fact manner.

Frans continued. "That Jewish woman is due to give birth very soon. I understand the doctor would rather not help with the delivery." It was an assumption Frans made, as he was worried that he would not be able to get any doctor's help.

"What?" the doctor's assistant responded with a puzzled look on his face. "If that's the case, then I will do it. I'll talk it over with him. When the time comes, I'll be there."

Frans was also worried that the doctor would not like the idea of having the birth take place in the convent, and he feared if he talked about the plan too much the doctor would talk Mother Superior out of allowing it. He knew doing the delivery within his own home was too dangerous.

As it turned out, a few days before the birthing, Frans ran into Dr. Baptist on the street. The doctor told Frans that he was fine with the arrangements being made, especially with the nursing sister being on hand to assist. He said that he would gladly help.

Sure enough, the doctor and his assistant were both present at the delivery. On February 10, 1944, Engelien Baars gave birth to a baby girl at the convent. She stayed a few days afterward to recover. Lou Baars visited his wife and baby daughter every day, usually at night. Agnes also visited once, and on the way back in the pitch dark, she rode her bike accidentally off the Maas Dike. But fortunately she was not injured.

A few days later, mother and child came home to the Wijnakker residence. No further major medical help was needed. The doctors did not come again. Mien stayed home for a week as if she was recovering from the childbirth.

Frans registered the birth as being his and Mien's own child. The official at the registry office congratulated him, and together they had a drink of Dutch gin.

Ina, called Ineke, Wijnakker was given the additional non-Jewish names of Francisca and Corrie, named after Frans Wijnakker and Cor van Doorn. She grew quickly and often stood outside in a baby carriage.

A few weeks later, Mien took the baby to the medical office for a checkup. Hanneke Peerboom, a woman from Haren, was there. She told Mien that the baby looked exactly like Nel (short for Petronella), Mien's mother. There was not a single suspicion.

Leah Sophia Ina Baars, the baby's real name—otherwise known through her Dutch identity as Ineke Francisca Corrie Wijnakker, usually just as Ineke—came into the world under difficult circumstances. But now, in essence, she had two sets of loving parents.

Chapter Twelve: Placement Challenges

The work of finding Dutch locals to take in Jews and hide them in their homes continued nonstop for Frans throughout the latter months of 1943 and well into 1944. In making these arrangements and keeping them working safely, Frans encountered constant challenges along the way.

For instance, the doctor from Megen, Dr. Baptist, was called in to see Engelien Baars's mother, Sophia Roselaar, when she got very sick. She was now hidden in another home near the Wijnakkers and was already in her seventies.

During the illness, Frans prepared for her eventual demise. She would be buried in the cemetery belonging to the ruined church next to the Wijnakker house. He had been to the notary public in Ravenstein to research whether there were still descendents of the people who had been buried last in that graveyard. There were none.

The family had died out. She would have been buried in the dark, and no one would know.

Luckily the preparations were not needed. Lien's mother survived the illness, as the medicine the doctor provided helped cure her.

Then there was the challenge in trying to get the cooperation of Piet Adriaans. Frans had been observing the house of Piet Adriaans for quite awhile. It was placed against the incline of the Maas Dike. Piet had a large house and was not home much. He lived alone and seldom had visitors come to his house. From its location and Piet's situation, his home would be a safe place for hiding Jewish refugees, Frans thought. Whether Piet would be willing to help was another story.

At the same time, Frans needed to find new arrangements for a Jewish couple from the town of Oss, Mr. and Mrs. Zwanenberg. They were hidden in another part of Oss. One evening, as Frans bicycled there to check in on the couple, he saw from the outside of the house Mr. Zwanenberg sitting in a circle of light in the living room. His dark features, along with his hat, made him an easily recognizable Jewish man. Dutch Christians did not wear hats when indoors while more devout Jewish men did so, either with a derby hat or with a yarmulke, the Jewish skullcap. On top of that, Zwanenberg, having been a resident of Oss, was very well known in the area.

When Frans went inside the house, he exclaimed to Mr. Zwanenberg, "How can you be doing something like that!"

"Only good people come here," Zwanenberg replied.

"But this house is along a main thoroughfare. People can see you easily here."

"Well, no, they don't know me," Zwanenberg tried to explain. "You know me, but you are nuts if you think that you have to be afraid that I'd be recognized."

"Be careful!" Frans warned as he left.

✳

Sure enough, one month later there was a letter in the mailbox of the home where the Zwanenbergs were being kept. The note demanded that some money be placed behind a certain tree by the following night, or the secret would be exposed.

Panic and worry ensued, and the decision was made for the Zwanenbergs to leave right away and go to Dieden. The thinking was if this hush money was paid, more would be asked for in the future.

So the Zwanenbergs, a couple in their fifties, were given directions on how to walk the long distance to the Wijnakker residence in Dieden. They arrived around midnight, exhausted from all the walking. They had not walked so much in a very long time. Because Frans was expecting them, a bed was made ready. They stayed for a while at the Wijnakker home. Mrs. Zwanenberg was always very scared. When a new person arrived to be hidden, she needed to know exactly who that person was, as she was terrified it could be a spy.

Frans wanted to find another place to hide them, and Mrs. Zwanenberg pleaded with him to do so as well. She told Frans, "Would you please find another place, a place for just us two? That would be good. We would gladly pay for it."

"Yes, that will have to be," Frans replied. "How much do you want to pay?"

"That doesn't matter, even if it is one hundred guilders per week," Mrs. Zwanenberg responded.

That was an immense amount. Normal room rent was then three to five guilders per week.

As Frans discussed the matter with Mien, the house of Piet Adriaans came up.

Would he agree to hide them was the big question.

So Frans bicycled over the Maas Dike to see if he could convince Piet Adriaans to help. As he got closer to Piet's home, Piet was bicycling toward him from the opposite direction. Piet went all over the area to collect payments from people for their utility bills—"for the lights" was the common expression. He was a rather strange man who loved money.

Frans called out to him. Piet grabbed his ear as he was rather hard of hearing and yelled out, "Do you want to talk to me?"

"Yes," Frans answered in a raised voice. "I want to speak with you."

"What is it?" Piet asked as he stopped his bicycle.

"Piet, you are getting houseguests," Frans boldly announced.

"Houseguests? Strange people?" Piet responded in puzzlement.

"Yes, strange people from near The Hague, from Scheveningen actually," Frans said as he began to weave his story in hopes of persuading Piet to provide his home for a safe haven. Situated close to The Hague, Scheveningen was a well-to-do town and the top beach resort community in the country, located along the North Sea.

"Strange people! Well that doesn't work just like that," Piet shot back.

"You'll get them. There's nothing you can do about it. I went to city hall, and your name is at the top of the list. You live alone in that house of yours. You'll get a couple from Scheveningen. They are quite wealthy."

Due to the war and the Nazi occupation of Holland, especially in the major cities of Amsterdam, Rotterdam, and The Hague, conditions had led to some non-Jewish Dutch people being displaced and in need of shelter. So the idea that someone would be asked to take in a fellow Dutch citizen was not too farfetched.

The word *wealthy* caught Piet's attention. "Rich people, you say?"

"Yes, rich people," Frans emphasized. "In fact, you actually should move fast to be ahead of the people at city hall. You should take them in immediately. Then they can't make you take anyone else. Your house is then occupied. You wouldn't have any extra room."

"Yes, yes, but I don't know these people," Piet said with doubt coming across in his voice.

"But I know them," Frans stated confidently. "I can help you take care of everything."

"But to have to take people in, I'm not so sure."

Frans jumped right in, continuing his sales pitch. "They are respectable people."

"Rich people too," Piet said, thinking out loud. "What's their name?"

Frans thought for a moment. He wanted to give a name that sounded good. "Schaffelaars," he said. "Let me check on what's happening with them, and I'll be back in touch with you in a few days to get the arrangements set."

❋

A few days later he met up with Piet Adriaans again.

"So what is their name? Didn't you say Schaffelaars? Wasn't that the man who jumped from the tower?" Piet asked.

"He is dead, but they're from that family," Frans quickly responded.

"Yes, respectable people. I have to be able to count on that. Are they Catholic?" Piet asked next.

"I haven't asked that yet. They could be Protestant," Frans said with a straight face.

"That doesn't matter," Piet said. "Then they have to go to Batenburg to the church there. But now something else. Come and see what they will have at my house."

"Good," Frans said. "They will live at their own expense. But they won't be bringing any furniture or other things with them. They'll have to use your things."

Frans did not want to tell Piet that he would have to cook for them. Then he might not agree to take in the couple. And, of course, he steered clear of mentioning they were Jewish.

When Frans came inside the house, he saw most of what Piet had was old junk.

"Here's a whole row of pots and pans that they can use," Piet said as he showed Frans around. "Come with me. Here's the bedroom. There is a feather cover on the bed that was my mother's. It is nice and warm. There are blankets, and there are the sheets. They can use it all. And there is the stove. They will keep it all clean, won't they?"

"They will keep it all clean," Frans answered. "You don't have to worry about that."

"Yes, I have to be able to count on that. I don't have a housemaid. You can understand that," Piet said.

"No problem," Frans said. "The woman is not that old. She'll keep everything clean."

"How old are they?" asked Piet.

"Around fifty or so," answered Frans. "How much were you thinking to charge them for that room? Say one hundred guilders for two rooms? That is a whole lot of money."

"That is a lot of money," Piet agreed. "But if they are rich people, it could be a bit more, couldn't it?"

"What were you thinking?" Frans asked.

"Make it one hundred twenty-five guilders," stated Piet.

"Piet, what would you do with that much money? I would be ashamed to have to ask for so much. These are good people."

"Yes, but if they have money anyway?" Piet pleaded.

"I'll try," Frans said. "Tomorrow evening I'll come to let you know."

✳

The next evening Frans returned. "I went to see the couple. They would like to come as quickly as possible, next week already."

"Yes, what did you agree on?" asked Piet.

"Piet, you said one hundred twenty-five guilders, but I did not dare say that, so I said one hundred guilders per week."

"Yes, I'll be all right with that," Piet responded. "Did you tell them they would be in a very nice place?"

"Yes, I said that." Frans nodded.

"That they will be in a fashionable home?" continued Piet.

"Yes, I told them that you are a distinguished man in a fashionable house," Frans stated without cracking a smile.

"Yes, yes. Do you know what religion they belong to?" Piet asked next.

"No, I didn't ask that yet. That doesn't matter anyway. I think they are Protestant so they'll go to Batenburg across the Maas River to church."

"They do have to go to church," Piet said emphatically.

"Yes, I know that, and they will do that I'm sure."

"When will they come here?"

"This Monday."

"What time?"

"At four," answered Frans. Actually, Frans knew that a four o'clock arrival would not happen. For greater safety, moving people was done when it was dark, but he didn't want to say a late time that might seem out of the ordinary.

"But four won't be possible. I have to be on my way home early. I can't just stay home, you know. Money does not grow on my back. I have to go to Schaijk (a local town a few miles south of Ravenstein). But if I know for sure they'll arrive at four, I'll quit early and catch up the next day."

"Yes, we'll be here at four o'clock," Frans stated.

"Then I'll be home at four," Piet said. "And how is it with the money?"

"They'll pay ahead of time. They'll give you one hundred guilders every week."

"Agreed," Piet said with a smile. "Honestly, they are honorable people?"

"Yes, you can count on that," Frans said. "They will pay you well, and you will do well from them. I know that for sure."

"Well, I don't want to lose anything by having them," Piet said as Frans departed.

*

Frans then went to the Zwanenbergs to explain the situation. "Listen to me a minute. I have found something good for you. You will do very well, and the house is located in a good place. There is a large sweeping willow in front of the door, so no one can see in. The curtains are always closed.

There is never anyone at home, and no one will open the door. If someone does come to the door, you also don't have to open the door. Do not say that you are Jewish. There is no talking about that. You are Protestant, and if he talks about the church, you'll tell him that you are old and that Batenburg is too far away."

Mr. Zwanenberg agreed. His wife started to cry, especially upon hearing they couldn't even say that they were Jewish.

"No, he must not know that," Frans continued. "Not at all! You'll also have to do the housework, but I will see to it that you have everything you need—food and everything else."

"When can we go there?" Mrs. Zwanenberg asked. It was Thursday at the time.

"Next Monday already," answered Frans. "I have settled everything. But he is greatly interested in money. He's doing it for the money; otherwise, he wouldn't do it. One hundred guilders is a lot of money, and you will have to pay for the food in addition to that. But there is no other possibility. If you want to have a good place, you'll have to go there. I'll see to it that you get enough to eat. There are pots and pans as well as a bed."

✳

On that Monday, Frans made arrangements with a cab driver in Dieden to pick up the couple and take them to Piet Adriaans' house, dropping them off after 8:00 p.m. when darkness would settle in. The driver was also instructed to take their suitcases inside the house before departing.

In addition, Frans told the driver what to say when he arrived at Piet's house to explain the late arrival. Frans knew that Piet tended to go to bed before 8:00 p.m. and that the house would be totally dark, as Piet wanted to pay as little as possible for electricity. Frans also assured the cabdriver that he would be nearby just in case.

When the cabdriver arrived that Monday evening just after eight, Frans was there, watching outside from the corner of the house. The cabdriver knocked continually harder, as Piet was hard of hearing and asleep. Finally he awoke.

"Heh, what's going on?" Piet shouted as he came to the door.

The driver, following Frans's instructions, said loudly behind the front door, "There were two people at the station, a man and a woman. The train had been delayed. Now they stood at the station in the dark, and they did not know the way. They have to come to your house. Wijnakker took care of that, right?"

"Boy, oh boy, it's starting already. You cannot trust that man," grumbled Piet. "It's already after eight."

"But I couldn't do anything else," the driver pleaded loudly.

"Yes, I'll have to pull on my pants, and then I'll be there," said Piet.

When Piet opened the front door, the driver, as instructed by Frans, took the suitcases inside and then left immediately.

It was dark outside. In addition, everything had to be kept dark due to the war. No lamp could be lit while the door was open. Piet Adriaans lit a lamp anyway. He then saw the man with a derby hat on his head and right away suspected the couple was Jewish.

He started to grumble loudly at the couple. "That awful Wijnakker. He told me that you were from The Hague, but you are Jewish. You are Zilverbergske, the shoe king! I also know your sons. You are the shoe king!"

Mr. Zwanenberg said nothing. His wife began to cry.

"You don't have to cry," Piet said as he began to simmer down. "But that awful Wijnakker. He tricked me. You'll have to leave at six tomorrow morning and return to Wijnakker. I hope you'll understand. I don't want any Jews. I'm not going to let myself be hanged. You'll have to sit in the front room. If they come, I'll say you arrived tonight. I'm going to bed now. I have to work again early tomorrow morning."

Standing out of view at the corner of the house, Frans had heard everything. The whole situation had gone wrong. He felt very sorry for these people. Depressed, he returned home. He did not really know what to do.

At home he talked about the dilemma with Mien. "Tomorrow morning at six they'll be back in front of our door. Everything went badly."

"Did he know them?" Mien asked.

"He did not know them," Frans replied, "but he thought he did. He thought they were the Zilverbergskes."

They discussed the matter for a little while. Then Mien suggested, "Go and speak about the situation with Piet's brother Bertus. He is much wiser. Maybe he is already aware that houseguests might have been coming to his brother's. Then let Bertus talk with his brother. Maybe they'll be able to stay anyway."

"They won't be able to stay," lamented Frans. "But sure, I'll go see Bertus anyway."

At Bertus Adriaans's place, one only had to knock once. He was not hard of hearing like his brother Piet or early to bed either. He answered the door quickly upon hearing the knock. Bertus engaged Frans in about a minute of small talk, asking Frans about how his meat trading business was going. He didn't know Frans was out of that business. Frans then asked if he could come in to discuss a problem.

Frans walked into the kitchen. Bertus's wife, Ton Arts, from Haren, stood up when she heard a familiar voice and warmly greeted Frans.

Bertus and his wife were aware that Piet had agreed to take evacuees from near The Hague into his house for one hundred guilders a week. Bertus said, "I told Piet that one hundred guilders is much too much. But he said, 'Wijnakker said it's okay. One hundred guilders are not too much. They are rich people who come from Scheveningen, so they can afford it.' He found that fine, as otherwise he would have had to take other evacuees into his house. Then you don't know who will be in your house. That's how he was talking."

Frans then explained what happened when the couple arrived at Piet's house and his refusal to want to keep them. Bertus asked their name.

"Zwanenberg," Frans said.

"From the large factory in Oss?"

Zwanenberg was the largest meat producer in Oss. Frans explained, "This man is not him but a nephew."

Frans continued, asking for Bertus's assistance. "If you would go to your brother Piet tomorrow morning early, a bit before six, as he wants to put the family on the street. If you would try to talk to him to let the couple stay, maybe it would help."

"I'll do that," Bertus agreed. "How about I come by and get you at four forty-five, and we can go together?"

"That's fine, but listen a minute. I won't go into Piet's house with you; otherwise, he'll start in on me. He'll be complaining that I am worthless, and he doesn't want any sorry Jews. You would not get a chance to talk. I'll listen outside at the window. He is so hard of hearing and talks loudly. I'll be able to hear everything."

Bertus agreed. "That's good. I'll go inside, and you'll stay outside."

Early the next morning, Bertus and Frans went to Piet's house. The door was unlocked. Piet had just gotten up. He was making himself some bread for breakfast. He looked up when he saw Bertus walk in and asked, "Is something going on?"

Bertus, at that time, worked for a milk producer. He drove a horse and wagon to pick up milk cans from farmers. "No, I just came for a visit," Bertus said.

"Or maybe you know something," Piet said. "I'll tell you! That ugly Wijnakker with his people from The Hague. There, behind that door are Jews. I'm not going to have Jews here. You can understand that!"

"Do you know who the Jewish man is?" Bertus asked.

"Yes, Zilverbergske from Oss," Piet answered.

"No, man, not Zilverbergske. But he is from the large factory in Oss. His name is Zwanenberg," Bertus explained.

"From that large meat factory?" Piet asked.

"Yes," Bertus said. "You've got to keep him and his wife. You have to give lodging to them. They really need your help. Don't let them do any work. Just tell them how much you want to charge because they will have enough money."

"They are from that large factory. How do you know that?" asked Piet.

"Frans Wijnakker told me."

"Darn it! Should I do it?" Piet wondered out loud.

"Yes, man. You'll do well by it," said Bertus reassuringly.

Bertus left and nodded at Frans that everything would be fine. Frans sighed in relief.

Piet Adriaans then knocked on the door of the room where the couple sat. "Come out. Money doesn't grow on my back. I have to go to work. My brother Bertus was here, and he said you were the family from the large factory in Oss. You can stay here as lodgers. You'll have to take care of yourselves. In the mornings, you'll get bread, and then I'll leave for work. Evenings I'll be home at five, and then you'll eat at six."

During the middle of the day, they got nothing to eat. Piet had no idea that they might want to have some lunch or drink a cup of tea. Piet was not generous. When Frans checked in at a later time, Piet told him, "They seem to be quite satisfied. In fact, this morning the woman was even singing. I think they're happy to be with me. I did not know that Jews could also be good people, but they are. Wijnakker, you and your friends from Oss, not The Hague, are decent people. I also learned that they are not the Zilverbergskes as I first thought. They are related to that family from the big factory."

✳

Frans visited the couple regularly. At Christmastime, he provided a big chicken. Mrs. Zwanenberg then cooked a fine Christmas dinner for Piet that she and her husband shared in.

A few days later when Frans stopped by, Piet Adriaans enthusiastically talked about his Christmas dinner experience. "I was sitting there waiting, dressed in my Easter best. I had returned from Mass, and at noon she called me to come and eat. Frans, not one spoon but two. There was also a fork and a knife and two plates, one on top of the other. All were clean and washed. Yes, it was all very formal. I've never had such delicious soup. She can cook! And the chicken, it was so very delicious, and we also had beans and pears. You are the one who must have brought the chicken and the other things. Right?"

"Yes, I brought it." Frans smiled.

"That's what I thought. I thought the Wijnakker must have done that. Did they ask you for that?" Piet inquired.

"No, I did that because it was Christmas."

"Is that so? Boy, did I eat delicious food. We ate it up. We ate it all up. In one meal, in one day. That whole chicken would have been enough for them for a whole week. We practically could not finish it. It really would have been enough for them for a whole week."

"Yes, but Piet it was Christmas," Frans reminded him.

The Zwanenberg couple stayed at Piet Adriaans's home until the end of the war, even though they usually had a fairly meager existence.

✳

Another placement challenge Frans had to deal with was right near his own home. Diagonally across from the Wijnakkers was a farm where the Van Camp family lived. Frans had asked whether they would be willing to hide an older man in their attic. They agreed to do so.

The arrangement was for this Jewish man to go upstairs and not come down—not for anybody. Everything was to be provided for him in his room up in the attic, which the man was fine with, as this provided for the most safety.

After the man had been staying at the Van Camp home for some time, one day the father of the house had a birthday party. Cookies were baked, and everyone was having an enjoyable time together. Mr. Van Camp thought that all the doors were shut and no one could come in.

As the party was going on, Mr. Van Camp said to his oldest son, "Why don't you get that man from upstairs? He sits there all alone all the time. No one will come, and every door is locked."

The oldest son went to get the man hiding in the attic. "Sir, please come on down. It's my father's birthday. We'd like you to come join us."

The man hesitated at first but went along with the request. As a religious Jewish man, he still always wore a yarmulke on his head. He joined in the party, having some coffee to drink and some cake to eat. He found the occasion very pleasant.

Suddenly, without warning, an official from Ravenstein walked into the front room. Apparently the house was not locked. The official had come to collect the dog tax. In Dieden, almost no one paid that tax. He saw the man sitting with the yarmulke on his head but said nothing directly about that.

Mr. Van Camp had stepped away from the front room. The tax official then asked the Jewish man, "Do you have a dog?"

"No, we have no dog," the man replied.

Suddenly a dog jumped out of a basket.

"And what about this one?" inquired the official, pointing at the dog.

The man answered, "Oh, he just walked in. It's not mine. But go ahead and write him up." This was an attempt to get rid of the official. The oldest son who had been standing by and watching the interaction the whole time then went to the door to let the official out of the house.

The official then whispered to the son, "Do you know that is a Jew who is sitting inside with you?"

"No, that is an uncle of my father's, from Eindhoven," the son replied.

"No, that is a Jew," said the official adamantly, who then left.

The son then told his father what happened. The next day Mr. Van Camp told Frans, "Come and get that man as soon as possible because we were betrayed."

"How so?" Frans asked.

"The tax official from Ravenstein saw the man in hiding when he was joining us downstairs for my birthday party. He said to my son, 'You have a Jew in your house.'"

"Oh, that's not a bad official. Don't worry," said Frans, trying to reassure Mr. Van Camp.

Frans wanted to keep the Jewish man in the same place, but Mr. Van Camp did not dare any longer. Mr. Van Camp then exclaimed, "Look Frans, word will travel shortly to the authorities. Not only will they come to get this Jewish man, but they will come to get us. We've been betrayed! You've got to get this man out of here right away."

Seeing this panic ensue along with the exclamation of "betrayed" was neither the first nor last time Frans would encounter this challenge out of his network of helpers. Later that evening, the man arrived back at the Wijnakkers.

After that, Frans sought out one of Mien's brothers who lived in Megen. He had a small house up against the Maas Dike. Her brother was called Jan the Otter in Megen, although he probably had only caught one otter in the Maas River. He was faced with the possibility of having to go to Germany to work as a forced laborer unless he could find a job. He did find a job at a farm in Dieden, but that only paid ten guilders per week, which was not enough to live on.

In came Frans with the answer to Jan's problem. While visiting with Frans and Mien at their house one day, Frans said to him, "If you take in a lodger from me, I can get you the pay of thirty guilders per week."

"That's quite a lot," Jan responded.

"That man can and will pay you that much," stated Frans.

"There is something more involved here," added Mien.

But before she could finish explaining the situation, Jan jumped in and said, "Makes no difference to me even if the person is a Jew."

"And that he is," said Frans.

The man was then placed in Megen in Jan's house. He stayed in a little chicken coop in the attic that had been turned into a small room. It was two-by-two meters and could only be reached via a trap door. The wife of that man was still in hiding in The Hague. She could no longer stay there due to increased house searches by the Germans. So Frans went to get her. They went together on the train, making their first stop in Den Bosch. There was a lot of SS and police activity when they arrived there, so Frans decided not to take any chances by trying to go home that evening.

In Den Bosch, Frans had an address where he could go in an emergency. He and his refugee passenger were able to stay there for the night. The next day he took the woman to

Megen, to the house where her husband was hidden. They had a happy reunion. Together in that little chicken coop room they stayed safely.

A short time later, Frans went to visit them. Upon greeting Frans, the wife asked, "Could you bring that nice lady in Den Bosch some flowers?"

"When I get to Den Bosch again, I'll do it," Frans replied.

"Do you still remember where she lives?" she asked Frans.

"I still have a note with the address," Frans showed her. "I could find her again."

The woman smiled and then gave Frans ten guilders to buy flowers.

✱

"A note? What were you thinking!" Long John said sternly when he heard what Frans was planning to do. The Underground expressly forbid any of its operatives from carrying around any paperwork with addresses listed on it. "Dangerous play is always forbidden!" Long John said angrily.

But the couple stayed in Megen in the home of Mien's brother Jan until the end of the war. They were well taken care of, yet they never went downstairs.

When the area was liberated, the man still did not want to come downstairs. Only when Frans went to see him and explained that the Allies truly had freed the town did the man come down.

＊

Another placement challenge involved Frans's younger brother, Jos. On New Year's Day of 1944, Frans helped a nineteen-year old Jewish girl from Amsterdam to escape, Theodora Broekman, or Teddy as she usually went by. He even stayed over in Amsterdam one night, which was not part of the plan, to allow the girl to spend New Year's Eve with her parents before departing—a risky proposition. Frans had no way of calling Mien, so she was stuck at home worrying and hoping that he was not captured by the German authorities.

Luckily nothing happened. In the evening of New Year's Day, Frans arrived home with the girl. The people in hiding asked him all about what was going on in Amsterdam, from who was still there to who had been hauled away. As a few of the people started to go back to bed while others continued talking, the front doorbell rang.

Only strangers rang the front doorbell. Thus Frans thought immediately that he had been followed and was now about to be arrested.

The doorbell rang only once, hard. Everyone quickly got into the hiding place. They stood close together, including the newly arrived Teddy. Frans made one more quick inspection to see that all were well hidden. No one could see that there was a hatch leading into the hiding room. This took a couple of minutes. Frans became less worried when the ringing of the doorbell was not followed by any pounding on the door or on the window shutters. Then it would have been the Germans for sure.

Frans opened the door, and there stood his younger brother, Jos, someone he viewed as a good guy but wild. Sometimes out in the open market Jos would yell loudly, "All *moffen* have to leave!" *Moffen* are gloves, but it was also a somewhat insulting Dutch word for Germans. If any Nazi sympathizers, N.S.B.'ers, or Gestapo officers would be in ear-shot of such a remark, an arrest if not a beating could result.

"How can you do something like that while you know I have Jews in my house?"

"It took a minute too long to open the door," Jos responded quickly. "You have to train them better. You should be able to open the door immediately."

Jos had coincidentally seen his brother and Teddy step on the train in Den Bosch, the transfer point for returning to Ravenstein. Frans had the girl sit near him. He had first looked to see if there were any SS or German soldiers on the train. Jos told him what he saw and then said, "You shouldn't do that."

Frans had been instructed since the beginning of his special work not to sit near the person he was helping to hide when riding on the train.

Knowing now there was no danger at the door, everyone came out of the hiding place, including the new girl. "Do you have a good place for her yet?" Jos asked while pointing to Teddy.

"Not yet, but I'll find one tomorrow or the day after," Frans replied.

"I know a good place. One you'd never find," Jos offered.

"In Haren?" Frans asked.

"No, somewhere else by good people. They'd never find her there."

"Oh? So where?" Frans asked. He was doubtful.

"Best to let her go with me, to my house," Jos stated. Jos still lived with their mother.

Frans then turned to Teddy and asked, "Do you want to go with him? He is my brother. Staying in his house means you can stay with my mother tonight. My sister also still lives there."

"Fine," answered Teddy.

✱

A few days later, Frans visited his mother to check on how all was going with Teddy. "Did Jos come here Sunday evening? He had a girl with him, right?"

"Yes," his mother responded. "That explains it. He must have gotten her from you. Then everything is okay. I thought she was a Jewish girl."

"Where is she now?" asked Frans.

"She's in back, in the kitchen. She can stay here. But Jos really shouldn't have known about this girl. He's already gone to see the priest."

"To see the priest?" a startled Frans blurted out. "What would he have to do there?"

"He was trying to talk the Father into allowing the girl to go with us to church on Sunday and to receive communion, with bread as a substitute. This way the people in town won't see her as Jewish since it looks like she goes to church. The Father would have nothing to do with it," explained Frans's mother.

When Jos came into the living room and heard his mother's explanation, Frans turned to him and said in a stern voice, "You can't do this sort of thing. The priest doesn't have to know about what's going on here with this girl."

Teddy continued to stay with Frans's mother for the time being.

❋

A month later when Frans came to visit his mother again and check in on Teddy, he found his mother to be the only one at home. She explained, "Your sister Annie went to Oss."

"And the girl?" asked Frans.

"She went with Jos to The Hague. I hated them going there, but what could I do?"

"With a Jewish girl to The Hague. What in heaven's sake did he have to do there?" Frans wondered out loud.

"He had two thousand guilders' worth of food coupons, and she is carrying them to help him out. Jos wanted to give her a little outing. Otherwise, she just sits here all day."

Frans's mother did not realize how dangerous that was. Teddy did not have a legal permit to be traveling around. Frans was very worried. What if the girl were to be arrested? She had seen everything in his house and could betray all if forced.

"She has to leave here," Frans told his mother.

Luckily, nothing happened while Teddy was with Jos in The Hague. A short while after she returned, Frans had Teddy moved away. He would not let Jos be involved again.

She was placed near the town of Oisterwijk with a good family. The father was an engineer. They had a son who studied in Tilburg. Teddy was well taken care of, but she was not allowed to go outside. That was punishment for this lively girl.

One day the parents were invited to attend the graduation of a young doctor. They had their son stay home with Teddy, their so-called daughter, to make sure everything stayed safe. When the parents returned home that evening, the light in the house was out, and the beds had not been slept in. They began to worry that the two young people had been hauled away. At 2:00 a.m. Teddy and their son finally came home.

"Boy, you have let us sit here terrified that something had happened to you!" they exclaimed.

"No need to worry. We just went to Tilburg to the movie theater."

The wife realized that her son and so-called daughter were starting to get involved with each other. Cor van Doorn received a telegram a short time later that said, "My son is in love with that girl. She is a sweet and pretty girl, but that cannot be allowed. I will take another younger girl in my house, but this one has to leave."

When Frans was notified, Teddy was moved out of Oisterwijk. She went to hide with a couple who had no children in a town north of Brabant province, Vlaardingen.

Frans strongly stressed for her to stay upstairs in her room. He was aware how hard that was for her.

As it turned out, had Theodora Broekman been able to stay in Oisterwijk, freedom would have arrived for her in September 1944 when the Allied forces liberated the southern part of the country. She would not have had to endure the so-called Hunger Winter, a period of suffering for occupied Netherlands during the winter of 1944 and 1945. During this winter, the Nazis blocked most food transports to the civilian population in the major cities in the west, as they were desperately fighting to hold off the Allied forces. At least twenty thousand Dutch civilians died of starvation that winter. The Allies did not liberate Vlaardingen and the rest of Holland until the end of the war in May 1945.

＊

Like Teddy, there was another Jewish young lady who found hiding especially difficult. She was from the Gosschalk family, the younger sister of Eva Hess. She wanted to live and felt stifled in hiding. She had arrived in a milk tank truck, which was used to sneak people out of the cities once it became too dangerous to walk on the streets. Inside the tank was also milk.

Frans brought the girl to a village across the Maas River. She had a legal permit that allowed her to go outside like other Dutch citizens, which was easier to arrange since she was a blond. She was placed at a cafe owner's house whose wife was sickly.

In setting up the arrangements for the Gosschalk girl, Frans applied his usual salesmanship with the cafe owner and his wife.

He asked the wife, "Don't you have any help?"

"No, it is so difficult these days. It's almost impossible to find help," she replied.

Frans spoke up readily. "I can help you with that. I know of a girl who is smart and hard working. She may be a little boy crazy, but they are all like that at her age. She comes from Amsterdam, and you'll even receive money for taking her in, ten guilders per week."

"You don't have to do that, providing us a girl to help out plus money. I don't understand that at all."

Frans reassured the cafe owner and his wife that this arrangement was a good deed for them to do. Shortly thereafter, Frans brought the young lady over. He explained to the couple, "Think carefully as you take care of this young lady. She does have a legal permit. She can be in the cafe to help out, but it is best that she not go outside. She knows not to say anything."

Initially the girl did well. The wife reported to Frans, "We are happy with her. We are lucky. You don't have to pay the ten guilders."

A short time later, Frans came for a visit to check to see how Mrs. Hess's sister was doing. Only the wife was home. "Where is the girl?" he asked.

"She went with my husband."

"What!" said an astonished Frans.

"After she finished her work, my husband invited her to bicycle along with him. That's allowed, isn't it?"

The woman did not know that the girl was Jewish. Frans thought it best not to say so. "Why does he do such a dumb thing?"

A month later Frans came by once again for a visit at the cafe owner's place. Again the Gosschalk girl was not there. Again she had gone out with the husband. The wife had grown suspicious in the meantime.

"Wijnakker, she is a good girl. I now know that she is Jewish, but please take her away. She's going out repeatedly with my husband. I don't know, and I don't dare say it out loud. I am sickly."

"Then she will leave," Frans stated. "You don't have to tell your husband anything. I'll say she has to leave. Don't let on. I'll come and talk to him tomorrow."

The next day Frans came by and said to the husband, "The girl has to leave here."

"Why?" he asked, looking puzzled.

"The organization (the Underground) has decided that this is for the best," Frans started to explain. "They are afraid that the girl will be picked up by the German authorities. When that happens, she will confess. This is for her safety."

If she betrays me, thought Frans, then the problems will be immense.

"But you'll get a new girl placed here," Frans said.

"Someone like her again?" the husband asked.

"I don't know yet," replied Frans. He then took the young lady and left.

She then was set up in a place near Tilburg. The family consisted of a couple with three children who could use help. They were strongly anti-German. They had a business, a carpentry shop. Business had dropped a lot during the war, and free help was welcome. As 1944 rolled on, liberation was in sight. The Germans were withdrawing to the north side of the rivers in the Netherlands.

There was a large attic above the business. They requisitioned it for quartering Allied troops and placed a sergeant and fifteen soldiers there. The girl also slept upstairs. There was a separate living space with a firewall that had a door that gave access to the rest of the attic.

One day an incident occurred, as the girl had seemingly agreed to a date with the sergeant. That evening the woman of the house heard noises.

"You're always hearings things," the husband said. "Go to sleep."

A bit later the wife woke him up again. "I do hear something!" she exclaimed.

"Yes, you're right," he said, as this time he could hear something going on too.

He went upstairs and saw the girl and the sergeant together, starting to get intimate. She had opened the fire door to let him in to her room.

Frans was notified and came by that day. He sternly said to the Gosschalk girl, "You know how dangerous that is. They picked up your mother, and you still do something like this."

The woman of the house said to Frans, "You told me she was a well-behaved girl. I see she's not. Take her with you. If she stays here any longer, we'll get betrayed."

Frans then took the young woman and went back to Dieden. When they arrived at his house, he told her, "You stay inside. Don't go out!"

"I want to go out," she protested. "I want to live. I want to go to Oss. I have a valid permit. If I can't go out..." She then looked down with tears starting to stream down her face. Frans knew that she did not recognize how dangerous the situation was, yet he could well imagine that the girl wanted to live.

"Self-discipline is necessary to stay alive," he said to her and left the matter alone from there. Eva Hess was there to also comfort and calm her younger sister. Luckily in September 1944 German forces had been pushed out of a southern section of the country, parts of Limburg and North Brabant provinces. This included Dieden. The Germans were still on the other side of the Maas River, not far away. While disaster with this nineteen-year old girl was averted for the moment and one could go outside a little easier now, full safety and freedom of movement were still precarious.

Chapter Thirteen: Not Always Successful

Not all of Frans's efforts to help provide refuge for Jews turned out successfully. Remembrances of those few incidents pained him.

For instance, one day Frans received a telegram from Cor van Doorn: "Small kitten. You are an animal lover. Could you come and pick it up?"

When he shared the telegram with Mien, she asked, "Should you do it?"

Frans decided to go ahead. At the given address in Amsterdam, he rang the doorbell. A woman who was about thirty years old asked from behind the door, "Are you here to pick up my child?"

"Yes," answered Frans.

Frans was let in and came upstairs. Then the child came into the room. She was very well dressed and was a beautiful girl of about three years old with black hair.

By her dark features, she was an easily identifiable Jewish child. When Frans saw the little girl, he was overcome with fear. He did not dare take her along. The girl could obviously not do anything independently due to her young age. In the train, they could not sit apart, as a three-year-old sitting on her own would look very strange and likely no young child would know how to sit alone quietly anyway. He could not suppress his thoughts that he would be picked up with the girl with all the dire consequences that could happen if arrested by the Germans, including for the people he had hidden in Dieden

Then Frans stated, "No, ma'am. I won't take her now, but I'll come for her tomorrow evening."

It was as if the woman realized that Frans had received a shock and was afraid to help out. In a desperate-sounding voice, she said, "Take her now please. I've already had to report to Vught. My husband is there also. There is somewhere I can hide, but I'm not allowed to bring my child. They can hear a young child."

The woman had been told that there would be no problem finding a hiding place for small children.

Vught was a small town near the city of Den Bosch in the southern part of the Netherlands. Camp Vught, built in the woods just outside the town in May 1942, was the one of the few Nazi concentration camps in the German occupied countries of northwestern Europe. Most of the concentration camps were in Poland and Germany with a few others sprinkled throughout parts of Eastern Europe.

"I'm not going home this evening but tomorrow evening," Frans explained. Frans then began to walk downstairs to depart. Pulling a chord from upstairs could open the outer door. The woman did not do that but came running down the stairs. She grabbed Frans's arm and begged, "Please take my child. Take her now please. It may be too late tomorrow."

"No, not tonight, tomorrow night," Frans said again as he opened the door and left.

He took the train home, and that evening talked the situation over with Mien. She said to him, "You disappoint me. Why didn't you take her with you as you had been ordered to do? Tomorrow is Sunday. Go get her Monday."

Frans agreed and went to Amsterdam that Monday to the same address. He rang the doorbell. No one opened. After a couple of rings, a neighbor said, "Do you need to go upstairs?"

"Yes," he said.

"Then you are too late," the neighbor responded. "The woman and the girl have been hauled away."

Frans always felt that he had not fulfilled his duty that time.

✳

In another instance, some time later in 1943, Frans was at the train station in Amsterdam. He saw a woman taking leave. She wore a star, the star the Nazis made Jews wear on their clothing when out in public. She had a young child with her and a number of suitcases. In the train station, Frans went to speak with her. She was going to Vught, she told him, to see her husband.

"It's far from sure your husband is still there," Frans said.

"I think he is," she replied.

"Lady, transfer to another train together with your daughter," implored Frans.

"Leave your luggage, and buy some new clothes. Otherwise you are lost."

"But I don't know you," the woman responded.

"That doesn't matter," Frans said. "You don't have to know me. I can help you and take you to a safe address."

"That's nice of you, but I don't dare," she said and walked away to her destination. Frans was left alone, unable to persuade the Jewish woman he could help save her.

Frans could also not help Roosje, a girlfriend of Freetje's from Amsterdam. Freetje had given him a note to take to her friend. The note said: "We are doing well here. It is a small farm town. You should also come."

Passing notes was considered high risk. It was not supposed to be done, per instructions of the Underground.

Frans was going to pick up Roosje at a certain moment in Amsterdam. When he arrived, her suitcases were packed and she was ready to leave. Saying good-bye to one another was very difficult for the family. Then doubt overtook her parents. They began to question if sending Roosje away was against God's will. *Shouldn't we wait and accept what God wants from us?* they wondered. The doubt led to Roosje staying. Frans went back home alone. Roosje and her family were later deported, but eventually she survived the war.

One last regret Frans had from all his efforts during the war directly involved Freetje, as described in Chapter Six. While his memory of what happened faded over the years and differed from what Shula (Freetje) reported, the fact of the matter was she was sent away from the Wijnakker home for a short while. She was able in the end to make her way back to Dieden where she remained with the Wijnakker family until the end of the war—much to the delight of Mien and Frans.

Chapter Fourteen:
The Threats and
Real Dangers

Frans and Mien Wijnakker always lived under a state of tension. Upon notification by the Dutch Underground, Frans was often traveling by train to Amsterdam and other cities to pick up Jewish refugees and find them safe haven in the south—a very risky business. On top of that, of course, they hid Jews in their own home, so the threat of a raid always hung over their heads.

There were also stories in the news of what happened when the SS caught members of the various resistance groups. Arrests and imprisonment were certain, and, in many cases, executions resulted. In fact, acts of sabotage to attacks on German authorities and those involved in the NSB were met with brutal reprisals by the SS—murders of many for the few of theirs that were hit, often including Dutch citizens with no direct involvement in the incidents at hand. The further and further Frans and Mien got involved in their special business, the more this tension and deadly risk hung over their heads.

Occasionally Frans would take on a risk as a favor for local people he knew. For instance, a short while after Ineke was born in February 1944, Frans ran into the local doctor, Dr. Sluiters, on his way about town.

"How's it going? It all went well, heh?" Dr. Sluiters inquired, referring to the birth of baby Ineke.

"Yes, everything went very well," Frans replied.

Then the doctor said, "Wijnakker, you really are carrying quite a load on your shoulders."

"Yes, that's true, but it is going well," Frans responded in a matter-of-fact manner.

"Well, since you are already so loaded down, could you save something for me?" Dr. Sluiters asked.

Frans thought the item in question was likely a pistol or something like that. He said to the physician, "I could if it is not too big."

"No, you can put it in your pocket. I shall go get it quickly. Will you hide it carefully?" the doctor asked.

"Sure, that is fine. I can help you out," Frans reassured the doctor.

Dr. Sluiters came back a few minutes later with a tile on which was painted *Je Maintiendrai*, the statement of resistance and independence shown on the Dutch national coat of arms. Symbols of Dutch nationalism were forbidden under Nazi occupation.

He explained to Frans, "Yes, they watch doctors carefully. Maybe my house will be searched by the Germans."

Frans came home with the tile, which Mien boldly hung on the wall in the living room. The Wijnakkers already had another Dutch tile on their wall, one originally made in Delft, a city a few miles southeast of The Hague known for its great tile making. Next to that was a photograph of the Dutch royalty. It would certainly draw attention during a house search by the Germans.

In the meantime, people in Dieden knew that there was something going on at the Wijnakkers' place. No one spoke about it out loud, but they did talk about it among themselves. The few times the word *Jew* was uttered, it was probably by chance. Those not directly involved in what Frans and Mien were doing did not actually know what was going on—not for sure at least.

The local people just found it strange that one couldn't enter the Wijnakker house without ringing the doorbell. In their friendly little village, as throughout the small towns in the area, all doors were usually left unlocked. They tried to find out more by asking Mien, whose main response was that it was fine that no one could just walk in their home.

In fact, a butcher from Oss came one day to the Wijnakker house. The butcher, who had done business with Frans before, had not come in a long time because Frans had told him he could not take any more meat from him. "After the war, you'll be welcome again," had been Fran's message to him.

The front door was locked as always. The butcher had to ring the bell, which was different from before when he used to just walk in. That puzzled him. One of the women in hiding, Eva Hess, also from Oss, recognized the butcher as he was coming up to the house. Some of the other Jewish residents had been sitting inside the house when the doorbell rang. They quickly went into the hiding place so they would not be seen.

"You're probably selling food coupons?" the butcher asked Frans after he opened the front door, trying to figure out what was going on.

"Yes," Frans answered.

"That's what I thought. You're surely going to Amsterdam?"

"Yes."

"You were probably counting them, and that's why the door was locked?" the curious butcher asked.

Frans smiled and then took over the conversation. "How is it going with the Jews in Oss?"

"All hauled away," the butcher replied.

"Is that right?" Frans replied.

A number of people were named after that.

"Mrs. Hess, she was an analyst of something?" asked Frans.

"She's been taken away."

"Also Zwanenberg?"

"Yes, him also," the butcher answered. "He drowned himself in Oyen. Didn't you hear that? It was all in the newspaper. His wife too."

The people in the hiding room could listen along with Frans because the butcher spoke rather loudly. When the butcher went away, they expressed pleasure in hearing that the word in Oss was that they had all been transported away.

People in Dieden tended to whisper and gossip about the Wijnakkers: "Did you hear? Some people are hidden," or, "I saw Frans going to visit someone," or, "There are curtains covering the windows all the time."

But if a stranger from out of the area came into town, the out-loud speculations and whispers ceased. Then it was quiet. The people they may have seen in hiding who sometimes were out and about in town were just visitors from the cities. They were at the Wijnakkers to recover from their illness was the story told.

This indirect support for Frans and Mien was invaluable, especially as the war started to turn in 1944 against the Germans and their presence in the south started to increase. No locals had any inclination to share any news or gossip with the German authorities.

Nonetheless, Frans and Mien became very careful with whom they talked to in the local area about what they were doing. In particular, there was a big difference between Frans's mother and Mien's mother. Frans's mother, Maria Wijnakker, could keep a secret, but Mien's mother, Petronella van de Coolwijk, or Nel, couldn't.

In particular, every day the baker came by the house of Mrs. van de Coolwijk. The worry was that if he was to ask if there was anything new going on, if she knew, she would likely blurt out that her daughter had a house full of Jews, so don't tell anyone. Therefore, Frans and Mien agreed that Mien's mother couldn't know anything of what went on in their house.

If, on an occasion, both mothers were together in Dieden, the visit had to be organized well ahead of time. For example, occasionally on her visits Mien's mother would see a good number of pots and pans on the stove. She would ask Mien, "Are you canning again?"

"Yes, it's the best way to save," Mien would answer.

While Mien's mother saw all those pots and pans with food on the stove, in the main room the table was set for the immediate family and the two grandmothers.

After the meal on such visits, Frans's mother, Maria Wijnakker, would tell Nel van de Coolwijk that she was used to taking a little nap in the afternoon. Then when she would go to rest in the bedroom a short time after the meal was over, Mien would take her mother for a walk and get some plums from a neighbor down the road. The people in hiding could then come out and eat, clean the dishes, and Frans's mother could have a pleasant time visiting with them.

Luckily for Frans and Mien the local people in the area were not threats to them. But they had other real threats to contend with, starting with the Ravenstein police chief. Chief van Meul tried to stick his nose into the Wijnakkers' business and tried to figure out what was going on. He had said that he wanted to know everything that went on in the community. He was suspicious of what was going on with Frans and certainly wanted to maintain the right appearances for the German authorities.

Frans felt intuitively that the man could not be trusted. In fact, one day in the early spring of 1944, Frans and Mien went together to Amsterdam. The police chief was also on the train, and he saw the Wijnakkers.

"Come sit with me for a moment," he said, motioning for them to come over.

Mien had a book in her hands and continued to read as if she did not hear him. Frans moved to sit by him.

"I've thought for months that you were dealing in food coupons or something like that," the chief said. "But maybe not; otherwise, I would have arrested you already. I don't see you as often as before, but two weeks ago—didn't your wife tell you?—I saw her carrying two heavy suitcases. *Heavy suitcases,* I thought. *Who does that to his wife!* I had her show me what was in them. They were filled with clothing, worn clothing and shoes. What do you need those for?"

"Oh, I exchange them sometimes. People here ask for clothing, and in Amsterdam you can get rid of anything," Frans replied.

"Oh, is that what you trade?" Chief van Meul inquired in a suspicious tone.

"Yes," stated Frans in a matter-of-fact tone.

"But that is not permitted," the chief emphatically said.

"According to you, nothing is allowed to be done anymore," Frans quickly responded. "But I will do what needs to be done."

"But there was Jewish clothing in the suitcases with a star that had been removed, but you could see that one had been there. It had faded," the chief said sternly.

Frans felt a shock. He had not known from Mien that the police chief had seen all this from her. As Frans would find out later in discussing the encounter with Mien, the chief actually had not let on to Mien about what he had seen at the time.

After thinking for a few seconds, Frans responded, "There couldn't have been a star on those clothes; otherwise, I wouldn't have picked up those clothes. But my wife collected that stuff in Amsterdam."

Of course, Frans and Mien knew the clothing was for the people hidden in Dieden and elsewhere.

"What are you going to do now in Amsterdam?" Chief van Meul asked a little more calmly now.

"Looking to see if I can earn something."

Chief van Meul's tone then changed, and he blurted out sternly, "Listen, you have a brother in Tilburg. I think that you go to Amsterdam to get Jews. I think that you travel during the days there and then return with them to Tilburg in the evenings. Then you take them to your brother, who sees to it that they go to Belgium, and then they find their way to Spain. You can earn a lot of money doing that. That's what I think you do."

The chief paused briefly and then continued, "But bear in mind, if I catch you doing that with Jews, those Shylocks, I'll arrest you. They once had the power in Germany where they could get away with lending money at such exorbitant rates to good people. Not anymore!"

Frans thought that the chief was close to knowing the truth about what he was doing. He responded smartly to the chief's rant with a question, "Can you then also earn money doing that?"

Chief van Meul shot back, "You know that! You know that very well. I see you travel by train so often."

Frans then excused himself and returned to sit next to Mien, who heard the exchange. He knew he had been threatened. He thought that continuing to come by train and potentially being seen walking with someone else would be too risky now. *From now on*, he thought to himself, *no one will arrive by train but via a milk tanker instead.*

Luckily for Frans, the police chief never caught him in the act. In fact, the chief, not long after their encounter on the train, was transferred to Boxtel, another jurisdiction in the province of Brabant, a good distance away.

✳

The Wijnakkers faced a couple of other threats that would affect their ability to help the people in hiding. First of all, the Wijnakkers were in danger of losing their house. They rented the house in which they lived. The owner was the Dutch Reformed Church, the largest Protestant faith in the Netherlands. Frans got along well with the manager of the church's properties. In the beginning of living in the house, in 1936, Frans had one-year leases. When the manager became aware he would be leaving, he recommended to Frans that he should take a long-term lease for twelve years. This was in 1939. This lease had been agreed upon. However, because of the German occupation, nothing was certain anymore.

Sure enough, in the late fall of 1943, Frans received notice that he would have to move out of the house soon. The process server said to him, "Wijnakker, be wise and move out. Those Germans will throw you out if you don't.

I will then have to put you out because a bailiff has to do that. You've got two weeks."

The process server continued, "They've offered you another smaller house. Go along with that. Save the contract you have. Then you'll be able to move back in after the war. The man who wants to live in your house is risking a lot anyway." The man who was to be given his house was not someone Frans knew. The suspicion was he was an NSB'er or some kind of Nazi sympathizer.

Frans did not talk about having people hidden at his house. He knew this process server from Oss fairly well but not well enough to be able to take him into his confidence. He, therefore, could not tell him that the house being offered was totally unsuitable because he would not be able to have space to hide anyone there.

Frans then went to see an attorney who he knew about in Den Bosch. This attorney was considered completely trustworthy and was known to have strong loyalties to the Netherlands. He said about the same thing as the process server—that moving out might be the best option, until Frans spoke about having a house full of hidden Jews. Frans was then asked to give a few names of the people in hiding.

After hearing a few names, the attorney jumped in and said, "Stop. I know enough. Something needs to be done."

The attorney made an appointment for the following evening with a judge in Den Bosch. At the meeting, Frans also had to explain what was going on exactly in Dieden and how essential it was that he continue to be the renter.

Procedures continued against the Wijnakkers. Frans even saw the man who wanted to live in his house leave a few times for Den Bosch dressed in his Sunday best. Frans himself did not need to appear again in Den Bosch.

A short time later, he was notified that the Reformed Church would rest its case. Frans and his family could stay in the house. Frans concluded that the judge managed the procedure in such a way that the proposed renter gave up on his attempts to free the house so he could move in.

One big worry was over. Frans never spoke with the hidden Jews about this potential danger so as to avoid any panic from happening.

A few months later, after the ordeal with the house was over, came another serious threat. Frans received notice that he would have to go to Germany as forced labor because he did not appear to have a regular job in the Netherlands. This was a very real danger. During the course of the war, some three hundred fifty thousand Dutch citizens were taken and forced to work in the fields and factories in Germany to help support the production of its military needs. Working conditions in Germany were harsh, and later in the war the factories became targets for Allied bombing raids. As mentioned in Chapter Four, thirty thousand Dutch citizens who went to work in Germany did not come home alive from the experience, and some came home disabled. Once the Dutch learned what forced labor in Germany entailed, that was not a job assignment anyone wanted. This notice presented a major obstacle to Frans.

Frans was still in service by Meulemans in Ravenstein. In the beginning of the war, a number of the nonpermanent mill workers had been laid off due to a loss of work for the mill. Not Frans. He had a permanent position. Frans asked if a nonpermanent worker who was newly married could stay on in his place. Frans certainly had another occupation going.

The director agreed with the arrangement that Frans be kept on the company rolls so he could be called in to work as needed.

In the beginning of 1944, Meulemans needed more workers. A number had resigned or stayed home with a so-called illness—some of them dealt in food coupons. They earned more that way than working at Meulemans for a wage. Frans was called to come in to work, but he did not go.

A short time later, Frans received notice that he was soon going to be called up to go and work in Germany. Frans sought the help of a friendly priest he knew from the town of Berghem near the city of Oss, Father Van Oekel. The priest said that he would try to get permission from the authorities for Frans to be able to stay at home. Looking unemployed and not having a good reason for not working would make one a prime target to be sent into forced labor.

Frans didn't hear anything for a short while and thought that everything was in order. Not so! He received a letter from Meulemans saying that if he did not show up for work right away they would report him to the employment office. That happened. The notice, referred to as Refuses to Work, went out. A few days later, he received a notice to report to the employment office in Oss.

One of the hidden Jews in the Wijnakker house, Eva Hess, had good contacts in Oss. She was a friend of the wife of Dr. Fontein, a physician in Oss. She helped Frans compose a letter to take to Dr. Fontein. When Frans went to see the doctor, he and his wife were amazed that their friend was hidden so close by. Dr. Fontein then told Frans to report to the hospital in Oss. An appointment was set for him to see a Dr. Vetter the next day at nine in the morning.

But when Frans arrived at the hospital, he had forgotten the name of the doctor he was supposed to see. Behind the counter sat a nun who asked him, "Who are you here to see?"

"The doctor," Frans replied.

"Which doctor, the supervising medical officer?"

"I don't think so. I need to see the regular doctor," Frans answered.

"So where did you work?" the nun asked.

"Meulemans," said Frans.

"Go sit on that bench. I'll check out who you're supposed to see." The nun thought that Frans was possibly retarded. He also had no medical coverage.

A few minutes later a man wearing big glasses appeared and said, "Is there someone here named Wijnakker?"

Frans spoke up, "Yes, that's me."

"Come inside and undress," the doctor said. It was Dr. Vetter, who knew about Frans's situation. The doctor examined Frans for a while and afterward dictated something to his secretary.

He then asked Frans, "Wijnakker, do you ever have stomach problems?"

"No, not really," Frans answered with a curious look on his face.

"Those Wijnakker types," the doctor said. "I've already seen a few of them like you, and all of them have stomach problems."

Afterward Frans got a letter from Dr. Vetter who told him to deliver it to the medical officer who was in his office at that time. The medical officer read the letter and said, "It does not look good for you."

"No?" a puzzled Frans said.

"I'll give you a note to take to the employment office. Come back here in ten weeks. If your stomach bothers you before then, come back sooner. There won't be any monitoring. You can go anywhere. You are also allowed to bicycle."

Frans then took the note to the employment office in Oss. His card was stamped. He was deferred from working in Germany—a big relief.

✻

Some time later, Frans ran into the managing director of Meulemans on the road.

"Wijnakker, are you sick or aren't you?" the boss asked. "I see you bicycling around the area sometimes."

"No, but I'm not allowed to work," Frans responded.

"You understand, I'm sure, that you are still our employee," the director said. "But you don't work. People might think that Meulemans is not cooperating with the authorities, and then we would be picked up." The boss did not say anything directly, but he wondered if Frans was doing something suspicious.

"You take too much on yourself." He then handed Frans a twelve-week wage packet, the benefit for his disabling illness.

✷

The biggest threat the Wijnakkers faced was the constant potential of a house raid by the Germans. The people in hiding were well trained that when the front doorbell rang, they were to quickly move into the hiding place. In fact, one time when the doorbell rang, it turned into a lesson for the Wijnakker children on what they should do and not do when a potential house search happened.

On this particular day in early 1944, the person ringing the doorbell was a local policeman sympathetic to what Frans and Mien were doing. He had come to warn them of a possible raid he heard that may be coming their way in the near future. When he rang the doorbell, the Jewish residents scurried into the hiding room—all except Sophia Roselaar, the mother of Engelien Baars. She happened to be in the bathroom at the time. Five-year-old Nellie, the Wijnakkers' eldest child, started knocking hard on the bathroom door and shouted, "Grandma, you've got to hurry! Someone is at the door. You've got to hurry and get into the hiding room!" Little Nellie, of course, was just trying to help.

The policeman could hear Nellie's warnings and smiled at Frans as they spoke briefly. After he departed, Mien pulled

Nellie aside and slapped her across the face. She sternly said to her daughter, "You must never say anything when someone is at the door. It is not safe. You must be quiet!" Nellie learned her lesson and never forgot it.

In another instance, an advanced warning was given of a raid to come at night. So on that night, all the people in hiding left the Wijnakker home and hid out for a while on the dike overlooking the Maas River. Frans came out later and told everyone that all was clear, but they did not know that no raid had actually occurred.

For the most part, during the war and occupation of Holland, German military forces and the SS were not seen too much in the rural areas of the country. They had a heavy presence in the main cities of the country. As the war wore on and Allied forces were advancing through Western Europe in 1944, the German presence began to show up more in the south. This led to two actual house searches with which the Wijnakkers and their refugees had to contend.

In one raid, a couple of SS men rang the bell and pounded on the front door. Within two minutes, everyone had scurried into the hiding room, and Frans opened the door. The men barged in saying little other than they needed to search the house. They then walked through each room of the house, banging on the walls with billy clubs and stomping on the floors. Little Nellie Wijnakker stared down at their shiny black boots, not wanting to look up and show the frightened look on her face. She feared that if the SS men saw her face, they would know something was wrong and all would be lost. Frans, meanwhile, remained calm and offered the SS men some sausage and beer.

They declined his invitation and then looked at the nationalistic tiles on the living room wall, including the one from Dr. Sluiters that Mien had hung up on the wall. On one of the other tiles inscribed in Dutch was the line: *If you have a motherland, don't cling to another, be neither Prussian nor British, be Netherlands.* Mien also had a photograph of Princess Juliana and Prince Bernhard, part of the Dutch royal family, up on the wall. They made no remarks about the tiles but asked about the photograph.

"Who is that?" asked one of the Germans, pointing to Juliana.

"My sister. Can't you see that?" Mien answered confidently.

A few moments later the two SS men left, saying no more than, "We may return."

Luckily Dr. Sluiters never had to visit the house and see where his tiles were hanging. Nor was he ever made aware of this raid.

※

The other raid, in May 1944, occurred while Mien was not home. She had gone to Haren to visit her mother. When Mien was on her way home, she was stopped by one of the townspeople who said, "Mien, should you really go home? I just passed your house, and there stood a large German car in front of your door. I also saw Germans getting out of it."

Mien felt forced to continue anyway, a knot in her stomach. A bit later she saw the car coming the other way. All kinds of fearful thoughts were present: *Are we betrayed?*

Are some of the Germans still in the house? Are they getting reinforcements?

She arrived home with her heart racing and exclaimed to Frans, "What happened?"

"Nothing really," Frans answered calmly.

"There were no Germans here?"

"Yes, they were here," he said and then went on to explain what just happened.

He had been sitting in the front room, visiting with Lou and Engelien Baars. Suddenly there was banging on the door. Frans saw a large car and German soldiers stepping out of it. He ran quickly through the house. Everyone had to go into the hiding place. He let the Germans wait a bit to make sure all was in order. Suddenly Engelien Baars knocked from the inside of the hiding room, and before Frans could react, she was already out.

"Woman, you have to stay in," he said to her.

She wouldn't listen and picked up her baby, who was about three months old and had been in a basket in the front room. Frans had tried to hold on to baby Ineke. But with the Germans pounding on the front door, he let go. The agreement in these situations was for the baby, who was registered as Frans and Mien's child, to be left outside along with the other Wijnakker children. Since a baby could cry during a house search, the thinking was everything would be much safer if she was left as is.

But Ineke Wijnakker was Engelien's child. Previous agreements about leaving the baby outside meant nothing in her panic. The child was pulled into the hiding room.

Frans then let the German soldiers in. "Eggs," they said in a short and insolent way. They had seen chickens walking outside. The Germans came inside, walked through the hallway that passed the stairs behind which the hiding place was located, and went in to the kitchen.

Frans had no eggs on hand at this time. He walked ahead of the Germans and guided them to the farmer across the street. He did have eggs. The Germans were satisfied and retraced their steps through the hallway to the front of the Wijnakker house again. The people in hiding had all heard the loud and quick passage of the Germans to and from the house. Luckily the baby was silent. Otherwise, all could have been betrayed.

Mien, while not happy about the risk Engelien Baars had taken, was relieved that nothing had come of this raid.

Chapter Fifteen:
The End
Finally Comes

Allied forces pushed the Germans out of the southern part of the Netherlands in mid-September 1944. The rest of the country was freed in May 1945 when the war in Europe finally came to an end with the defeat of Adolf Hitler and Nazi Germany.

Conditions were not fully safe initially in September 1944, as fighting was going on between German and Allied forces. In fact, while Canadian forces had come through the area of Brabant province where the Wijnakkers resided, giving people a sense of liberation, all territory north of the Maas River remained under German control until the full liberation of the country came in May 1945. So danger lurked close by to Dieden and its surrounding communities. As evidence of this, one day in late September Nellie and her brother Jan were out playing with Freetje along the dike of the Maas River. Overhead a firefight erupted between a German and an American plane, and a bomb dropped on the ground not far from where they were all standing. Freetje immediately pushed the two young Wijnakker children to the ground for protection. They landed in a field of nettles, prickly plants that scratched up their bare legs, and, while scared, they were otherwise unharmed.

Engelien Baars was coincidentally in Ravenstein at this time. She was on her way to the house of Marie Louise, where she had lived temporarily, to thank her. The whole center of Ravenstein got blocked off when news of some possible assassination hit. Engelien was able to find her way to the van Doorn house. Cor van Doorn had nine children of his own, but he gave her a night of shelter. Shocked by this experience, Lien returned the next day quickly to the Wijnakker house.

For the Jews who had been in hiding, the urge to go out was understandable. For those who came from nearby towns, they could return home shortly after the initial liberation. The others who came from the north and the west, which was still occupied until May 1945, stayed in Dieden but could at least go outside now.

When the war finally ended throughout the whole country, Avraham Laub, known as Fritsje, went to live in Oss. He later joined Shula, known as Freetje, and their sister Sara, eventually making their way to live in the post World War II newly formed nation of Israel.

Shulamit Laub would actually be the first from her family to move to Israel. She would sneak into then British-controlled Palestine with other World War II Jewish refugees in 1945. She had remained with the Wijnakkers through the end of 1944, not knowing what had happened to her other two sisters, Esther and Hannah. Mien provided her a bicycle so she could go search for them. She rode south, spent time in the city of Eindhoven, and after two months found Esther and then Hannah. Both sisters had spent the war hidden in Limburg, the southernmost province in Holland.

Saying good-bye to the children, including Agnes, was difficult for Frans and Mien. They had become like their own children—God's children, they often said to each other afterward. The departure of Freetje, now Shula, was probably the most emotional and tearful of the good byes for all involved.

Ineke Wijnakker got her real family name Baars from the courts. Leah Ineke Baars moved with her parents and her grandmother, Engelien's mother, after the war first to Amsterdam, where, in 1946, her brother Bernard was born, and then on to the city of Eindhoven in the southern tip of the province of Brabant about an hour south of Dieden. In late 1957, Lou and Engelien, later known as Lynn, moved their family to the United States and finished raising their two children in the Los Angeles area. Lou had a successful career as an architect.

Shula Laub would become Shula Schwarz, marrying Kurt Schwarz in 1952. They made their life in Haifa, Israel. She would become a nurse and go on to have three children, a very happy marriage, thirteen grandchildren, and (as of the writing of this book) three great grand children.

For Frans and Mien, the end of the war meant the end of a tense time. While not daring people, they had risked their lives over a nearly two-year period. They had started something that they could absolutely have not predicted the course it would take. But they stuck with that course, having up to ten extra people reside in their house and helping place a number of others in need of safe haven. In the end at least two dozen Jews had been helped and saved by Frans and Mien Wijnakker, and miraculously no one got caught.

In June 1945, their fifth and final child was born, a daughter named Irene. Frans had to go back to making a living again and just supporting his family. Frans and Mien had to get back to a normal life again and raise their family. Years later the Wijnakker children would remark how it took their parents at least six months to adjust back to a normal life after the war ended. They had lived on the edge for nearly two years and remarkably thrived on it.

Frans gave up the job of working at the mill. He went to work at a meat processor plant in Oss run by the Zwanenberg family, whose nephew he had helped find a hiding place. Not surprisingly, Frans stayed employed there until he retired. The family stayed in that Dieden house next to the old church and eventually took ownership of it. Frans, Jr. and his wife live in it still today. Through reconstruction done on the house, the hiding place no longer exists. Luckily it's not been needed since.

Many of the Jews who had been hidden continued to have contact with the Wijnakkers after the war. The Baars family, before immigrating to the United States, would usually have a summer visit each year with the Wijnakker family. After all, Ineke was like a younger sister to their four older kids.

The courage that Frans and Mien displayed was formally recognized by Yad Vashem, the Holocaust memorial museum in Jerusalem, in August 1983—posthumously for Mien, who had passed away in 1980. Yad Vashem recognized them as Righteous Among the Nations, the recognition for non-Jews who helped save the lives of Jews during World War II. The document that highlights their heroics says in part: "At the risk of their lives, they saved the lives of Jews during the Holocaust." In the document, Isaiah 56 was also quoted: "I will give them a name and a place that will last forever."

An olive tree was also planted for Frans and Mien in the grove outside of the museum building at Yad Vashem in the area known as the Avenue of the Righteous. Alongside it is a plaque with their names, Frans and Hermina Wijnakker.

Before Frans went off to Israel to accept this great honor in 1984, the local communities of Ravenstein and Dieden held a ceremony to recognize the courageous acts of Frans and Mien. Flying in to be on hand for this event in the summer of 1984 and riding along in the parade for Frans was a school psychologist now living and working in San Francisco who came with her then five-year-old daughter Shoshana. That psychologist was none other than Leah Baars, originally known as baby Ineke Wijnakker.

A few months after the local ceremony, thanks to some financial support from some of the people who had been hidden at the Wijnakkers, Frans was able to fly to Jerusalem and be honored in a ceremony at Yad Vashem. Among the attendees there to give support was a nurse who resided in Haifa, Shulamit Schwarz, otherwise known as Freetje.

As so many in Europe turned a blind eye or even participated with the horrific actions of the Nazis against Jews during World War II, Frans and Mien Wijnakker proved to truly be righteous people. As said in Yiddish, they were *mensches*—good quality people. Or as described by their daughter Irene, they set the example of how to lead a Christian life.

Chapter Sixteen:
Epilogue and
the Journey

Leah "Incke" Baars was in the parade during the summer of 1984 when the communities around Dieden honored their local hero Frans Wijnakker, now Righteous Among the Nations. She then went back home to San Francisco and continued a fine career as a school psychologist and adding a second daughter, Alana, into her life. But she and the Wijnakkers lost touch. Living continents away, raising families, and working, not hard to lose touch.

Then twenty-five years later, she convinced her new husband (the author of this book) to join her on an extended trip to her original homeland of the Netherlands. Along the way on this very enjoyable trip, curiosity got her. While Frans and Mien were no longer alive, Leah wondered if she could find and reconnect with any of the five Wijnakker siblings.

As described in the letter I wrote to Leah's daughters Shoshana and Alana in Chapter One, we reconnected. We met Frans, Jr. and his wife Irene, who live in the actual house in Dieden where their parents' rescue work occurred.

As we departed from that meeting on Monday afternoon, May 25, 2009, we were invited by Frans, Jr. and his younger sister Irene to come back Wednesday evening. They would see who they could get together.

What would happen? After all, we had shown up in the area unexpectedly, and people have busy lives.

Wednesday Evening, May 27, 2009

All five of the Wijnakker siblings came that evening. (Check out the picture of the happy renunion that evening.) With Ineke Baars suddenly in town, they were not going to miss the opportunity to see her again, some twenty-five years later.

We had a very nice visit with the Wijnakker children that evening at Irene's house, the youngest of the five children. As mentioned, the rest of the kids -- Nellie, Thijs, Jan, and Frans, Jr., -- were there, and three of the four who have spouses brought them too. (Mind you, these kids are in their sixties and early seventies now with children and grandchildren too.) Here we are showing up in town unexpectedly just a little over a day ago, and all five Wijnakker siblings come out because Leah "Ineke" Baars is here. Shows you the quality of people they are.

The conversations throughout the evening were lively and friendly. They caught up with Leah, and she with them. We learned a little more about the experience during the war, which we read in the self-published book about their parents. Interestingly enough, four of the children have traveled to Israel and have visited Yad Vashem while there, seeing the memorial plaque in the Avenue of the Righteous to their parents.

On their visits, they also caught up with Shula—known during the war to them as Freetje—who lives in Haifa. Now past eighty years of age, she was the first person Frans took into hiding during the war when she was a child of fourteen. We also learned that at their local church when the kids go through communion, they are given the self-published book about Frans and Mien Wijnakker and told to use it as an example of how to lead a Christian life.

While I could participate little in the conversations directly since none of the Wijnakkers spoke much English and, of course, I speak even less Dutch, I was never bored or feeling out of place. Leah would periodically translate and ask questions for me. The atmosphere was one of joy in being able to see Ineke Baars again. Watching this happy reunion take place was special.

After being there a few hours, we ended the evening with Leah translating a few words on my behalf. We mentioned that we finished the self-published book and enjoyed it, commenting their parents were real heroes. Then lastly we said they and their parents were all mensches and what that means in Yiddish—good quality people. They appreciated the comments.

THE JOURNEY SINCE

As this second edition comes out, I am now entering my sixth year of an unexpected journey of sharing this special story of rescue, some five hundred events since it started. I have been in a dozen cities for speaking events beyond my home base of the San Francisco Bay Area, some more than once. The storytelling presentations I deliver have been in a wide variety of venues:

* churches
* synagogues
* occasionally churches and synagogues together
* a couple of Muslim-based organizations
* universities
* community colleges
* middle schools and high schools
* libraries
* book stores
* workplaces
* professional conferences
* Rotary and Kiwanis clubs
* Holocaust museum
* history museum
* multiple types of social service organizations
* Hadassah groups
* people's homes
* retirement groups
* Jewish Community Centers
* even the Dutch consulate in San Francisco

I've led fascinating discussions with book clubs. I now do the same in some schools where the progressive teachers there have the students read the book first before I come to lead discussion. Some rich discussion has occurred, with a nice tradition built up with some schools where I return each year for a new class.

This unexpected journey continues for two main reasons: 1) the story itself. People find the story inspirational, and messages of doing the right thing, ethics, courage and compassion, and making a positive difference have resonated for many. 2) Supporters. I have gained a litany of supporters over the past few years, people who have spread the word and made connections for me to speak in their organization from places of faith to places of work and many others just mentioned. Thank you to the many supporters who have helped and encouraged me on the journey with this special story. Maybe as you're reading the book today, you may become one too.

I am fortunate to be the humble messenger for two real heroes, Frans and Mien Wijnakker.

When I do my storytelling presentations, most of the time the audience members attending have not yet read the book. What they hear up front is that I have a meaningful personal connection to this story and its heroes. I then reveal it in the very end, introducing the baby the Wijnakkers helped get born and kept safe—my wife Leah Baars.

I'll end this book the same way I end each presentation and book discussion after all the audience questions: Thank god for the courage and compassion of Frans and Mien Wijnakker.

Bibliography

Dawidowicz, Lucy S. *The War Against the Jews* 1933–1945. Bantam Books: New York, 1975.

Flim, Bert Jan and Michman, Jozeph, editors of Netherlands volume and Gutman, Israel, editor-in-chief. *The Encyclopedia of the Righteous Among the Nations: Netherlands, Rescuers of Jews during the Holocaust.* Yad Vashem: Jerusalem, Israel, 2004.

Herzstein, Robert Edwin. *The Nazis, World War II.* Time-Life Books: Alexandria, Virginia, 1980.

Maass, Walter. *The Netherlands at War:* 1940–45. Abelard-Schuman Limited: London, 1970.

Prosser, Dr. Jacob. *Ashes in the Wind: The Destruction of the Dutch Jewry.* Souvenir Press: London, 1968 and 2010.

Van Tongeren, W. J. M. *Few of the Few: Hidden People in Dieden*. BV Numij: Leiden, Netherlands, 1993.

Verzetsmuseum (Dutch Resistance Museum). Amsterdam, Netherlands.

Wolf, Diane. *Beyond Anne Frank: Hidden Children and Postwar Families in Holland*. University of California Press: Oakland, California, 2007.

MARTY BROUNSTEIN

CPSIA information can be obtained
at www.ICGtesting.com
Printed in the USA
FSOW03n1123290716
23195FS